MATH Trailblazers®

A BALANCED MATHEMATICS PROGRAM INTEGRATING SCIENCE AND LANGUAGE ARTS

Unit Resource Guide
Unit 8

Applications:
An Assessment Unit

THIRD EDITION

KENDALL/HUNT PUBLISHING COMPANY
4050 Westmark Drive   Dubuque, Iowa 52002

A TIMS® Curriculum
University of Illinois at Chicago

UIC The University of Illinois
at Chicago

The original edition was based on work supported by the National Science Foundation under grant
No. MDR 9050226 and the University of Illinois at Chicago. Any opinions, findings, and conclusions
or recommendations expressed in this publication are those of the author(s) and do not necessarily
reflect the views of the granting agencies.

Letter Home

Applications: An Assessment Unit

Date: _____

Dear Family Member:

So far this year, students have completed many laboratory experiments. In this unit, students complete a lab to assess their abilities to collect and analyze data while studying the life spans of people, animals, and soap bubbles.

This unit also includes several other assessments. Students read an *Adventure Book* about Florence Kelley, a social reformer who collected data on child labor. They write a report that displays and analyzes data she collected. They also take a paper-and-pencil test on skills and concepts learned since the beginning of the school year. At the end of the unit, students will add activities to their portfolios. They will review their portfolios comparing newly completed activities to old in order to show their growth in mathematics.

Students play a game to practice multiplying decimals.

As we work through this unit, you can help your child by doing the following activities at home:

- Ask your child to tell you about the *Adventure Book*.
- Play the game *Three in a Row* with your child after he or she has played it in school.
- Help your child practice the multiplication and division facts using the *Triangle Flash Cards*. Your child's fluency with these facts will be assessed as part of this unit.

Thank you for your support.

Sincerely,

_____

Carta al hogar

Aplicaciones: una unidad de evaluación

Fecha: _____

Estimado miembro de familia:

Durante este año, los estudiantes han tenido muchas oportunidades para completar experimentos de laboratorio. En esta unidad, los estudiantes harán un experimento para evaluar sus habilidades para colectar y analizar datos a través del estudio de la duración de la vida de las personas, los animales y las pompas de jabón.

Esta unidad también incluye varias evaluaciones más. Los estudiantes leerán un *Libro de Aventuras* sobre Florence Kelley, una reformadora social que colectó datos acerca del trabajo de niños. Los estudiantes escribirán un informe que presenta y analiza los datos colectados por Florence Kelley. También tomarán un examen de papel y lápiz acerca de las habilidades y los conceptos que aprendieron desde el comienzo del año escolar.

Los estudiantes juegan un juego para practicar la multiplicación de decimales.

Al final de la unidad, los estudiantes agregarán actividades de esta unidad a sus portafolios. Revisarán sus portafolios y compararán las actividades recién completadas con las más viejas para mostrar su avance en las matemáticas.

A medida que trabajamos en esta unidad, usted puede ayudar a su hijo/a haciendo las siguientes actividades en casa:

• Pidiéndole a su hijo/a que le cuente sobre el *Libro de Aventuras*.

• Jugando el juego Tres en fila con su hijo/a después que lo haya jugado en la escuela.

• Ayudando a su hijo/a a practicar las tablas de multiplicación y división usando las *tarjetas triangulares*. El dominio de las tablas se evaluará como parte de esta unidad.

Gracias por su apoyo.

Atentamente,

_____   _____

Table of Contents

Unit 8
Applications: An Assessment Unit

Unit 8

Outline
Applications: An Assessment Unit

Unit Summary

Estimated Class Sessions 9-14

This unit applies and expands concepts and skills learned in the first seven units. Assess students on these concepts and skills as they work on the activities and labs. They demonstrate their knowledge by solving problems that arise in several contexts that have strong connections to science and social studies.

Students review labs completed in the first half of the year in preparation for completing the assessment lab, *Comparing the Lives of Animals and Soap Bubbles.* As part of the lab, students apply their knowledge of percents and interpret graphs.

They also read the Adventure Book *Florence Kelley,* which describes the work of a social reformer in the late 1900s who—through data collection—was able to contribute to the passage of child labor laws in Illinois. This Adventure Book sets the stage for an assessment activity called *Florence Kelley's Report* in which students interpret Florence Kelley's data as she reported it to the governor.

This unit includes the *Midyear Test* and a portfolio review session. The DPP for this unit tests all the multiplication and division facts.

Major Concept Focus

- experiment review
- interpreting data tables and graphs
- portfolio review
- binning data
- *Adventure Book:* child labor
- communicating solution strategies
- midyear test
- representing quantities using fractions, decimals, and percents
- estimating products of decimals
- point and bar graphs
- TIMS Laboratory Method
- percents
- Student Rubric: *Telling*
- Student Rubric: *Knowing*
- multiplication and division facts

Pacing Suggestions

This unit will take 9 to 14 days to complete. It includes a variety of review and assessment activities that allow teachers to assess individual growth in mathematics as students continue learning while applying concepts and skills in new contexts.

- Lessons 2 and 7 are optional lessons. Lesson 2 *Three in a Row* is a challenging game that provides practice estimating with decimals. Lesson 7 *Review Problems* is a set of word problems that reviews skills and concepts from the first seven units. You can assign these problems for homework. Lesson 7 is also appropriate for use by a substitute teacher.

- Lesson 3 *Florence Kelley* is an Adventure Book story that provides a strong connection both to language arts and social studies. It sets the stage for the open-response assessment problem in Lesson 4 *Florence Kelley's Report.* Allow two days for Lesson 4 if you plan to let students revise their responses. Alternatively, you can use language arts time for students to read the story or write and revise their responses.

- Lesson 5 *Life Spans* and Lesson 6 *Comparing Lives of Animals and Soap Bubbles* provide connections to science. Students can collect data for the lab in Lesson 6 during science time.

Assessment Indicators

Use the following Assessment Indicators and the *Observational Assessment Record* that follows the Background section in this unit to assess students on key ideas.

A1. Can students collect, organize, graph, and analyze data?

A2. Can students make and interpret bar graphs and point graphs?

A3. Can students translate between graphs and real-world events?

A4. Can students use numerical variables?

A5. Can students choose appropriate methods and tools to calculate (calculators, pencil and paper, or mental math)?

A6. Can students solve open-response problems and communicate solution strategies?

A7. Can students use fractions, decimals, and percents to represent the same quantity?

A8. Do students choose appropriately whether to find an estimate or an exact answer?

A9. Do students demonstrate fluency with the multiplication and division facts?

Unit Planner

KEY: SG = Student Guide, DAB = Discovery Assignment Book, AB = Adventure Book, URG = Unit Resource Guide, DPP = Daily Practice and Problems, HP = Home Practice (found in Discovery Assignment Book), and TIG = Teacher Implementation Guide.

	Lesson Information	Supplies	Copies/Transparencies
Lesson 1 **Experiment Review** URG Pages 26–36 SG Page 270 DAB Pages 135–136 DPP A–B HP Part 1 *Estimated Class Sessions* **1**	**Activity** Students review experiments completed in the last seven units in preparation for the assessment lab in this unit. **Math Facts** Complete DPP Task B, which reviews multiplication and division facts. **Homework** Assign Part 1 of the Home Practice. **Assessment** Use the *Observational Assessment Record* to note students' abilities to organize, graph, and analyze data.	• student portfolios	• 1 transparency of *Distance vs. Time Graph* URG Page 34 • 1 transparency of *Experiment Review Chart* DAB Pages 135–136 or large sheet of paper for a class chart • 1 copy of *Observational Assessment Record* URG Pages 11–12 to be used throughout this unit
Lesson 2 **Three in a Row** URG Pages 37–41 DAB Pages 137–139 *Estimated Class Sessions* **1**	OPTIONAL LESSON—ENRICHMENT MATERIAL **Optional Game** Students play a game that involves estimating products of decimals. **Math Facts** Remind students to practice their facts at home using their *Triangle Flash Cards*. **Homework** Have students play the game at home.	• 8–10 game markers or tokens of one color per student • 1 calculator per student	• 1 transparency of *Three in a Row* game board DAB Page 139
Lesson 3 **Florence Kelley** URG Pages 42–52 SG Pages 271–272 AB Pages 47–60 DPP C–D HP Part 5 *Estimated Class Sessions* **1**	**Adventure Book** Students learn about the life of Florence Kelley, who helped reduce child labor in Chicago around 1900. They use data she collected to make predictions. **Math Facts** DPP item C practices multiplication and division facts using variables in number sentences. **Homework** 1. Assign DPP Task D, which provides practice with estimation and operations. 2. Assign Part 5 of the Home Practice, which reviews reading and interpreting data in a bar graph. **Assessment** Use Lesson 4 *Florence Kelley's Report* to assess students' abilities to analyze and display data as well as communicate mathematically.	• 1 calculator per student	• 1 transparency of *Increase in Work Done: Third Annual Report* URG Page 50

	Lesson Information	**Supplies**	**Copies/Transparencies**
Lesson 4 **Florence Kelley's Report** URG Pages 53–68 DPP E–F *Estimated Class Sessions* **1-2**	**Assessment Activity** Students use the Adventure Book in Lesson 3 to demonstrate their abilities to graph and analyze data. They describe their conclusions in writing. **Assessment** 1. Compare this lesson to work on *Stack Up* in Unit 2. 2. Assess students' abilities to work cooperatively. 3. Use DPP item F to assess students' abilities to communicate mathematically.	• 1 calculator per student	• 1 copy of *Florence Kelley's Report* URG Page 66 per student • 1–2 copies of *Centimeter Graph Paper* URG Page 67 per student • 1 copy of *TIMS Multidimensional Rubric* TIG, Assessment section • 1 transparency or poster of Student Rubric: *Knowing* TIG, Assessment section • 1 transparency or poster of Student Rubric: *Telling* TIG, Assessment section
Lesson 5 **Life Spans** URG Pages 69–82 SG Pages 273–275 DAB Page 141 DPP G–H HP Part 2 *Estimated Class Sessions* **1-2**	**Activity** Students compare human life span data from 1858 to life span data from 1997. They organize and graph the data, scaling the vertical axis using percents. **Homework** 1. For homework, students can complete the data table and graph for 1997 data. They find the median age at death for this data. *(Questions 9–12)* 2. Assign Part 2 of the Home Practice.	• 1 calculator per student	• 2 copies of *Centimeter Graph Paper* URG Page 67 per student • 1 transparency of *Graphing Life Spans* URG Page 80, optional • 1 transparency of *Life Spans Data Tables* DAB Page 141, optional
Lesson 6 **Comparing Lives of Animals and Soap Bubbles** URG Pages 83–96 SG Pages 276–279 DAB Page 143 DPP I–N HP Parts 3–4 *Estimated Class Sessions* **3**	**Assessment Lab** Students collect data about the life spans of soap bubbles. They compare this data to the life spans of animals. Students scale the vertical axis using percents. **Math Facts** DPP items I, K, and M review math facts. **Homework** 1. Assign some or all of the review problems in Lesson 7 for homework. 2. Assign Parts 3 and 4 of the Home Practice. **Assessment** 1. Grade the lab by assigning points to drawing the picture, collecting and recording the data, graphing, and solving problems. 2. Score student responses to *Questions 10–12* using the Telling dimension of the *TIMS Multidimensional Rubric*.	• 1 small jar of bubble solution per student group • 1 bubble wand per student group • 1 stopwatch or watch that measures seconds per student group • 1 calculator per student • paper towels	• 1 copy of *Centimeter Graph Paper* URG Page 67 per student • 1 transparency of *Soap Bubbles Data Table* DAB Page 143, optional • 1 transparency of *Centimeter Graph Paper* URG Page 67, optional • 1 copy of *TIMS Multidimensional Rubric* TIG, Assessment section

(Continued)

	Lesson Information	**Supplies**	**Copies/ Transparencies**
Lesson 7 **Review Problems** URG Pages 97–103 SG Pages 280–281 HP Part 6 *Estimated Class Sessions* **1**	OPTIONAL LESSON—REVIEW MATERIAL **Optional Activity** Students solve word problems using ratios, decimals, and percents. **Homework** 1. Assign some or all of the problems for review, homework, or use for assessment. 2. Assign Part 6 of the Home Practice.	• 1 centiwheel per student • 1 ruler per student • 1 calculator per student	• 1 copy of *Centimeter Graph Paper* URG Page 67 per student
Lesson 8 **Midyear Test** URG Pages 104–116 DPP O–P *Estimated Class Sessions* **1-2**	**Assessment Activity** Students take a short item test assessing skills and concepts learned in Units 1–8. **Math Facts** Remind students to study for the *Multiplication and Division Fact Inventory Test*.	• 1 ruler per student • 1 calculator per student • 1 protractor per student	• 1 copy of *Centimeter Dot Paper* URG Page 108 per student, optional • 1 copy of *Midyear Test* URG Pages 109–113 per student
Lesson 9 **Portfolio Review** URG Pages 117–123 SG Pages 282–283 DPP Q–R *Estimated Class Sessions* **1**	**Assessment Activity** Students update and review their portfolios. **Math Facts** DPP item Q assesses the multiplication and division facts using an inventory test. **Homework** You can assign DPP item R as homework. **Assessment** Transfer appropriate documentation from the Unit 8 *Observational Assessment Record* to students' *Individual Assessment Record Sheets*.	• collection folders • portfolio folders	• 1 copy of *Multiplication and Division Fact Inventory Test* URG Page 25 per student • 1 copy of *Individual Assessment Record Sheet* TIG Assessment section per student, previously copied for use throughout the year

Connections

A current list of literature and software connections is available at *www.mathtrailblazers.com*. You can also find information on connections in the *Teacher Implementation Guide* Literature List and Software List sections.

Literature Connections

Suggested Titles

- Appelhoff, Mary, Mary Frances Fenton, and Barbara Loss Harris. *Worms Eat Our Garbage.* Flower Press, Kalamazoo, MI, 1993.
- Cole, Joanna. *The Magic School Bus: Lost in Space.* Scholastic, New York, 1990.
- Littlefield, Cindy A. *Real-World Math for Hands-On Fun!* Williamson Publishing, Charlotte, VA, 2001.
- Schwartz, David M. *If You Made a Million.* Scholastic, New York, 1989.
- The EarthWorks Group. *50 Simple Things Kids Can Do to Save the Earth.* Andrews and McMeel, Kansas City, MO, 1999.
- Wilder, Laura Ingalls. *Little House in the Big Woods.* HarperCollins, New York, 2001.

Software Connections

- *Fraction Attraction* develops understanding of fractions using fraction bars, pie charts, hundreds blocks, and other materials.
- *Graph Master* allows students to collect data and create their own graph. (Lesson 6)
- *Math Arena* is a collection of math activities that reinforces many math concepts.
- *Math Munchers Deluxe* provides practice in basic facts and finding equivalent fractions, decimals, percents, ratios, angles and identifying geometric shapes, factors, and multiples in an arcade-like game.
- *Mighty Math Calculating Crew* poses short answer questions about number operations, 3-dimensional shapes, and money skills.
- *Mighty Math Number Heroes* poses short answer questions about fractions, number operations, polygons, and probability.
- *TinkerPlots* allows students to record, compare, and analyze data in tables and graphs.

Teaching All Math Trailblazers Students

Math Trailblazers® lessons are designed for students with a wide range of abilities. The lessons are flexible and do not require significant adaptation for diverse learning styles or academic levels. However, when needed, lessons can be tailored to allow students to engage their abilities to the greatest extent possible while building knowledge and skills.

To assist you in meeting the needs of all students in your classroom, this section contains information about some of the features in the curriculum that allow all students access to mathematics. For additional information, see the Teaching the *Math Trailblazers* Student: Meeting Individual Needs section in the *Teacher Implementation Guide*.

Differentiation Opportunities in this Unit

Games

Use games to promote or extend understanding of math concepts and to practice skills with children who need more practice.

- Lesson 2 *Three in a Row*

Laboratory Experiments

Laboratory experiments enable students to solve problems using a variety of representations including pictures, tables, graphs, and symbols. Teachers can assign or adapt parts of the analysis according to the student's ability. The following lesson is a lab:

- Lesson 6 *Comparing Lives of Animals and Soap Bubbles*

DPP Challenges

DPP Challenges are items from the Daily Practice and Problems that usually take more than fifteen minutes to complete. These problems are more thought-provoking and can be used to stretch students' problem-solving skills. The following lessons have DPP Challenges in them:

- DPP Challenge F from Lesson 4 *Florence Kelley's Report*
- DPP Challenges J and N from Lesson 6 *Comparing Lives of Animals and Soap Bubbles*
- DPP Challenge P from Lesson 8 *Midyear Test*

Journal Prompts

Journal prompts provide opportunities for students to explain and reflect on mathematical problems. They can help both students who need practice explaining their ideas and students who benefit from answering higher order questions. Students with various learning styles can express themselves using pictures, words, and sentences. Teachers can alter journal prompts to suit students' ability levels. The following lessons contain a journal prompt:

- Lesson 1 *Experiment Review*
- Lesson 3 *Florence Kelley*
- Lesson 6 *Comparing Lives of Animals and Soap Bubbles*

Extensions

Use extensions to enrich lessons. Many extensions provide opportunities to further involve or challenge students of all abilities. Take a moment to review the extensions prior to beginning this unit. Some extensions may require additional preparation and planning. The following lessons contain extensions:

- Lesson 2 *Three in a Row*
- Lesson 5 *Life Spans*
- Lesson 6 *Comparing Lives of Animals and Soap Bubbles*
- Lesson 8 *Midyear Test*

Unit 8

Background
Applications: An Assessment Unit

"To ensure deep, high quality learning for all students, assessment and instruction must be integrated so that assessment becomes a routine part of the ongoing classroom activity rather than an interruption."

From the National Council of Teachers of Mathematics *Principles and Standards for School Mathematics, 2000.*

The most powerful indicator of a student's new knowledge is whether he or she can apply that knowledge to new situations. This assessment unit provides many such opportunities. Students will demonstrate their understanding of concepts studied in the first half of the year by solving problems from several contexts that have strong connections to science and social studies.

Each lesson in this unit reviews, extends, or assesses concepts studied in the first seven units. Lessons 1, 2, 7, and 9 provide opportunities for reflection and review. In Lesson 1 *Experiment Review* students compare and contrast the labs they completed in the first semester. They consolidate their understanding of concepts and strengthen skills such as identifying variables in an experiment and making predictions from graphs. The second lesson *Three in a Row* is a game in which students practice and improve their skills estimating products of decimals. Lesson 7 is a diverse collection of word problems that review skills and concepts that are on the midyear test. In Lesson 9, students review and add to their portfolios. They compare work from the beginning of the year to their more recent work.

The remaining lessons give a balanced picture of students' learning by including an open-ended task in which students must communicate mathematically, a long task that takes several days to complete, and traditional tests that cover a wide range of content. These lessons parallel the assessment activities in Units 1 and 2 so you can evaluate students' progress since the beginning of the year. For example, in order to document improvement in students' communication skills, compare their write-ups of the problem-solving task *Stack Up* in Unit 2 to the reports they write analyzing data in Lesson 4 *Florence Kelley's Report.* Compare the lab *Searching the Forest* in Unit 1 and other labs to the lab *Comparing Lives of Animals and Soap Bubbles* in Lesson 6. The midyear test is made up of short items covering content from each unit, and the Daily Practice and Problems includes a test of the multiplication and division facts.

The diverse nature of the assessment activities in this unit reflects the balance of skills and concepts studied so far this year. The varied sources of information gathered in this unit will make your assessment of student progress more reliable. Significantly, the activities allow students to continue learning while providing multiple opportunities for them to demonstrate their mathematical knowledge.

Resources

- *Assessment Standards for School Mathematics.* National Council of Teachers of Mathematics, Inc., Reston, VA, 1995.
- Behr, Merlyn J., and Thomas R. Post. "Teaching Rational Number and Decimal Concepts." In Thomas R. Post (ed.), *Teaching Mathematics in Grades K–8: Research Based Methods.* Allyn and Bacon, Boston, 1992.
- *Principles and Standards for School Mathematics.* National Council of Teachers of Mathematics, Reston, VA, 2000.
- Stenmark, J. K., V. Thompson, and R. Cossey. *Family Math.* Lawrence Hall of Science, University of California, Berkeley, CA, 1996.

Observational Assessment Record

A1 Can students collect, organize, graph, and analyze data?

A2 Can students make and interpret bar graphs and point graphs?

A3 Can students translate between graphs and real-world events?

A4 Can students use numerical variables?

A5 Can students choose appropriate methods and tools to calculate (calculators, pencil and paper, or mental math)?

A6 Can students solve open-response problems and communicate solution strategies?

A7 Can students use fractions, decimals, and percents to represent the same quantity?

A8 Do students choose appropriately whether to find an estimate or an exact answer?

A9 Do students demonstrate fluency with the multiplication and division facts?

A10 _____

Name	A1	A2	A3	A4	A5	A6	A7	A8	A9	A10	Comments
1.											
2.											
3.											
4.											
5.											
6.											
7.											
8.											
9.											
10.											
11.											
12.											
13.											

Name	A1	A2	A3	A4	A5	A6	A7	A8	A9	A10	Comments
14.											
15.											
16.											
17.											
18.											
19.											
20.											
21.											
22.											
23.											
24.											
25.											
26.											
27.											
28.											
29.											
30.											
31.											
32.											

Unit 8

Daily Practice and Problems
Applications: An Assessment Unit

A DPP Menu for Unit 8

Two Daily Practice and Problems (DPP) items are included for each class session listed in the Unit Outline. A scope and sequence chart for the DPP is in the *Teacher Implementation Guide*.

Icons in the Teacher Notes column designate the subject matter of each DPP item. The first item in each class session is always a Bit and the second is either a Task or Challenge. Each item falls into one or more of the categories listed below. A menu of the DPP items for Unit 8 follows.

Ⓝ **Number Sense**	⊞ **Computation**	🕐 **Time**	◲ **Geometry**
D–G, J, K, N–P, R	D, F, K, L, P	N	A, H
⁵ˣ⁷ **Math Facts**	$ **Money**	⫿⫿ **Measurement**	⬚ **Data**
B, C, I, K, M, Q	O, R	A, H	J, R

The Daily Practice and Problems and Home Practice Guide in the *Teacher Implementation Guide* includes information on how and when to use the DPP.

Review and Assessment of Math Facts

By the end of fourth grade, students in *Math Trailblazers* are expected to demonstrate fluency with all the multiplication and division facts. The DPP for this unit continues the systematic approach to reviewing these facts. It reviews all five groups of facts—the 5s and 10s, the 2s and 3s, the squares, the 9s, and the last six facts (4×6, 4×7, 4×8, 6×7, 6×8, and 7×8).

DPP item B instructs students to quiz each other on all the multiplication facts using the *Triangle Flash Cards*. (One group of facts flash cards was distributed in the *Discovery Assignment Book*

following the Home Practice in Units 2–6.) After students sort the multiplication facts, they should record their progress on clean copies of the *Multiplication Facts I Know* chart. Then they should quiz each other on all the division facts and begin new *Division Facts I Know* charts. Ask students to compare their new charts with those they updated in Units 2–7. Since these new charts are a record of students' progress with the facts, have students place them in their portfolios.

Encourage students to practice only the facts not circled on their new charts. They can take home their *Triangle Flash Cards* or they can make a new set of cards for these facts using the *Triangle Flash Card Master*, which follows the Home Practice in the *Discovery Assignment Book*.

At the end of the unit, students take a test on a mixture of multiplication and division facts (see DPP Item Q). The test immediately follows the DPP.

Using the test results, students should update their new *Multiplication Facts I Know* and *Division Facts I Know* charts. Note: If a particular fact is not on the test (e.g., 4 × 3) but students correctly answered a related fact (12 ÷ 4), they may circle both facts on their charts. Throughout second semester, students can continue to practice those facts not yet circled on their charts by using the *Triangle Flash Cards*. Blackline masters of the *Multiplication Facts I Know* and *Division Facts I Know* charts are in Lesson Guide 2 of Unit 2.

For more information about the distribution and assessment of the math facts, see the TIMS Tutor: *Math Facts* in the *Teacher Implementation Guide*. Also refer to Unit 2 Lesson Guide 2 and the DPP guide in the *Unit Resource Guide* for Unit 2. All the *Triangle Flash Cards, Triangle Flash Card Master,* and *Facts I Know* charts are available in the *Grade 5 Facts Resource Guide*.

 **Daily Practice and Problems**

Students may solve the items individually, in groups, or as a class. The items may also be assigned for homework. The DPPs are also available on the Teacher Resource CD.

Student Questions	Teacher Notes

 Measuring Area

1. Rectangle ABCD has a length of 6 cm and a width of 8 cm. What is its area?

2. Rectangle JKLM is 20 cm by 4.8 cm. How many times greater is its area than rectangle ABCD?

TIMS Bit

1. 48 sq cm

2. two times greater; 96 sq cm

Multiplication and Division Facts

With a partner, use the *Triangle Flash Cards* to quiz each other on the multiplication facts. Have your partner cover the shaded number (the product). Use the two uncovered numbers to solve a multiplication fact. As you are quizzed, sort the cards into three piles: those facts you know well and can answer quickly, those you know using a strategy, and those you need to learn. Then, circle the facts you know well and can answer quickly on a clean copy of the *Multiplication Facts I Know* chart.

Next, quiz each other on the division facts. To quiz you on the division facts, have your partner cover the numbers in the circles first and then the numbers in the squares. Solve a division fact with the two uncovered numbers. Sort the cards and record your progress on a clean copy of the *Division Facts I Know* chart.

List the facts you have not yet circled on both your charts. Take the flash cards for these facts home so you can practice them. Your teacher will tell you when to expect the test on these facts.

TIMS Task

Students can take home the flash cards for the facts they need to practice, or they can make cards for those facts on copies of the *Triangle Flash Card Master,* which follows the Home Practice in the *Discovery Assignment Book.* Part 1 of the Home Practice reminds students to take home these newly prepared flash cards to study for the test.

The *Multiplication Facts I Know* and *Division Facts I Know* charts were distributed in the *Unit Resource Guide* for Unit 2 Lesson 2. See this Lesson Guide for more information.

Inform students when you will give the test on these facts. This test assesses students on multiplication and division facts. It is DPP item Q. A blackline master of the test immediately follows the DPP.

All the *Triangle Flash Cards, Triangle Flash Card Master, Facts I Know* charts, and *Multiplication and Division Fact Inventory Test* are in the *Grade 5 Facts Resource Guide.*

C Fact Practice I

Find n to make each number sentence true.

A. $5 \times 8 = n$

B. $3 \times n = 21$

C. $36 \div 6 = n$

D. $n \times 5 = 10$

E. $10 \times 4 = n$

F. $20 \div n = 4$

G. $12 \div 3 = n$

H. $9 \times 6 = n$

I. $n \times 8 = 64$

TIMS Bit

A. 40　　B. 7

C. 6　　D. 2

E. 40　　F. 5

G. 4　　H. 54

I. 8

D Practicing the Operations

Solve the following using paper and pencil. Estimate to make sure your answers are reasonable.

A. $62 \times 48 =$

B. $871 \div 6 =$

C. $36.3 \times 0.5 =$

D. $8243 - 738 =$

E. $21.8 \times 5 =$

F. $8.2 \times .47 =$

G. $76 \times 200 =$

H. $34 \times 800 =$

I. $8294 + 5088 =$

TIMS Task

A. 2976　　B. 145 R 1

C. 18.15　　D. 7505

E. 109　　F. 3.854

G. 15,200　　H. 27,200

I. 13,382

E Equivalent Fractions

Find the equivalent fractions.

A. $\frac{3}{5} = \frac{?}{10}$

B. $\frac{3}{4} = \frac{?}{12}$

C. $\frac{2}{5} = \frac{8}{?}$

D. $\frac{5}{10} = \frac{?}{2}$

E. $\frac{10}{12} = \frac{5}{?}$

F. $\frac{1}{3} = \frac{?}{12}$

G. $\frac{5}{9} = \frac{?}{36}$

H. $\frac{7}{10} = \frac{?}{100}$

TIMS Bit

A. $\frac{3}{5} = \frac{6}{10}$　　B. $\frac{3}{4} = \frac{9}{12}$

C. $\frac{2}{5} = \frac{8}{20}$　　D. $\frac{5}{10} = \frac{1}{2}$

E. $\frac{10}{12} = \frac{5}{6}$　　F. $\frac{1}{3} = \frac{4}{12}$

G. $\frac{5}{9} = \frac{20}{36}$　　H. $\frac{7}{10} = \frac{70}{100}$

F Wall Painting

Michael's family painted the living room and dining room walls. Michael painted $\frac{1}{8}$ of the walls. His sister painted $\frac{1}{4}$ of the walls. Dad painted $\frac{3}{8}$ of the walls. Mom finished the project.

Write three math questions you can ask about Michael's family project. Exchange your problems with a partner or present them to the class to solve.

TIMS Challenge

Answers will vary.
Sample questions:

What fraction of the work did Mom complete? ($\frac{1}{4}$)

Who did the most work? (Dad)

Who did the second most? (sister and Mom)

How much more did Dad do than Michael? ($\frac{2}{8}$ or $\frac{1}{4}$)

What fraction of the project was completed by the children? ($\frac{3}{8}$)

G Quick Change

Change the following fractions to decimals and then to percents.

A. $\frac{23}{100}$

B. $\frac{3}{4}$

C. $\frac{30}{50}$

D. $\frac{68}{100}$

E. $\frac{5}{10}$

F. $\frac{2}{8}$

G. $\frac{9}{100}$

H. $\frac{2}{40}$

TIMS Bit

Calculators should be available. Discuss students' strategies. For example, to change $\frac{2}{8}$ to a decimal, students can divide $2 \div 8 = 0.25$. Or, they can reduce $\frac{2}{8}$ to $\frac{1}{4}$, then write $\frac{1}{4} = \frac{25}{100} = 0.25$.

A. 0.23; 23%

B. 0.75; 75%

C. 0.6; 60%

D. 0.68; 68%

E. 0.5; 50%

F. 0.25; 25%

G. 0.09; 9%

H. 0.05; 5%

Slab-Maker Problem

You need a protractor and centimeter ruler to complete this task. Follow the instructions below to create quadrilateral CDEF.

Make side DE 5 cm long.

Make ∠D 95°.

Make side CD 7 cm long.

Make side EF 3 centimeters shorter than side CD.

TIMS Task

Answers will vary. One possible solution:

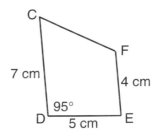

 Fact Practice II

Find *n* to make each number sentence true.

A. $10 \times n = 90$ B. $16 \div 2 = n$

C. $3 \times 5 = n$ D. $28 \div 4 = n$

E. $4 \times n = 36$ F. $50 \div n = 10$

G. $6 \times 2 = n$ H. $24 \div 3 = n$

I. $7 \times n = 63$

TIMS Bit

A. 9   B. 8
C. 15   D. 7
E. 9   F. 5
G. 12   H. 8
I. 9

J Letter Chances

1. Write down your full name (first, last, and, if you like, middle name). If you cut out all the letters in your names and put them in a bowl, list the probability of choosing each letter that appears in your name. For example, if your name is Roberto Ruiz, the chance of choosing an R is $\frac{3}{11}$. The chance of choosing an O is $\frac{2}{11}$. The chance of choosing a B is $\frac{1}{11}$.

2. What is the probability you will choose a vowel from the letters in your name?

3. What is the probability you will choose a letter in the first half of the alphabet (A–M)?

4. What is the probability you will choose one of the last five letters in the alphabet?

TIMS Challenge

Answers will vary.

Sample answers based on the name Roberto Ruiz.

1. Probability of choosing:

   R $\frac{3}{11}$; O $\frac{2}{11}$; B $\frac{1}{11}$; E $\frac{1}{11}$;

   T $\frac{1}{11}$; U $\frac{1}{11}$; I $\frac{1}{11}$; Z $\frac{1}{11}$

2. $\frac{5}{11}$

3. $\frac{3}{11}$

4. $\frac{1}{11}$

K Fact Practice III

Find n to make each number sentence true.

A. $70 \times 6 = n$ B. $90 \times 90 = n$

C. $3000 \div 6 = n$ D. $14{,}000 \div 200 = n$

E. $40 \times 400 = n$ F. $56{,}000 \div 80 = n$

G. $30 \times n = 180$ H. $5000 \times 9 = n$

I. $800 \div 10 = n$

TIMS Bit

A. 420   B. 8100

C. 500   D. 70

E. 16,000   F. 700

G. 6   H. 45,000

I. 80

Student Questions	**Teacher Notes**

 Adding and Subtracting Fractions

A. $\frac{3}{6} + \frac{2}{6} =$　　　　B. $\frac{2}{3} + \frac{1}{5} =$

C. $\frac{1}{4} - \frac{1}{6} =$　　　　D. $\frac{5}{8} - \frac{1}{4} =$

E. $\frac{3}{8} - \frac{1}{8} =$　　　　F. $\frac{1}{2} - \frac{2}{5} =$

TIMS Task

A. $\frac{5}{6}$　　　B. $\frac{13}{15}$

C. $\frac{1}{12}$　　　D. $\frac{3}{8}$

E. $\frac{2}{8}$ or $\frac{1}{4}$　　F. $\frac{1}{10}$

 Fact Practice IV

Find *n* to make each number sentence true. Then name one other fact in the same fact family.

A. $9 \times 2 = n$　　　B. $30 \div 5 = n$

C. $7 \times 7 = n$　　　D. $32 \div 8 = n$

E. $10 \times 7 = n$　　F. $6 \times 8 = n$

G. $27 \div 3 = n$　　　H. $8 \times 9 = n$

I. $24 \div 4 = n$

TIMS Bit

A. 18; $2 \times 9 = 18$;
$18 \div 2 = 9$;
$18 \div 9 = 2$

B. 6; $30 \div 6 = 5$;
$6 \times 5 = 30$;
$5 \times 6 = 30$

C. 49; $49 \div 7 = 7$

D. 4; $32 \div 4 = 8$;
$4 \times 8 = 32$;
$8 \times 4 = 32$

E. 70; $7 \times 10 = 70$;
$70 \div 10 = 7$;
$70 \div 7 = 10$

F. 48; $8 \times 6 = 48$;
$48 \div 8 = 6$;
$48 \div 6 = 8$

G. 9; $27 \div 9 = 3$;
$9 \times 3 = 27$;
$3 \times 9 = 27$

H. 72; $9 \times 8 = 72$;
$72 \div 8 = 9$;
$72 \div 9 = 8$

I. 6; $24 \div 6 = 4$;
$6 \times 4 = 24$;
$4 \times 6 = 24$

A Busy School Day!

1. On an average school day, Jackie spends six hours in school. What percent of her day is spent in school?

2. Jackie practices piano one hour on a school day. What fraction of the day does she spend practicing piano?

3. Jackie spends $\frac{1}{3}$ of a day sleeping. How many hours does she sleep?

4. What fraction of Jackie's day is left after school, piano, and sleep? More or less than $\frac{1}{2}$ of a day?

5. Write a similar story using your own daily activities.

TIMS Challenge

1. 25%
2. $\frac{1}{24}$
3. 8 hours
4. $\frac{9}{24}$; less than half
5. Answers will vary.

 Estimating with Money

Estimate the answers to the following problems.

A. $34.56 + $72.35

B. $0.39 + $1.76

C. $0.58 × 8

D. $275.34 − $56.23

Explain your strategy for B.

TIMS Bit

Estimates will vary.

A. over $100

B. $2.15

C. $4.80

D. $225

Possible response: 39¢ is close to 40¢ and $1.76 is close to $1.75. $1.75 plus 25¢ is $2.00. 40¢ − 25¢ is 15¢. Add 15¢ to $2.00 for $2.15.

Number Puzzles

A. I am 3 tenths less than 5 times 7. Who am I?

B. I am twice the sum of 3.4 and 2.1. Who am I?

C. I am less than 10 but more than 5. If you skip count by two-tenths (.2) starting at 0 you get me. The digit in the ones' place is the same as the digit in the tenths' place. My ones' digit is a multiple of 4

TIMS Challenge

A. 34.7

B. 11

C. 8.8

 Multiplication and Division Fact Inventory Test

Students take a test that contains the facts from all five groups of facts studied in Units 2–8—the 5s and 10s, 2s and 3s, square numbers, 9s, and the last six facts.

Students should have two pens or pencils of different colors. During the first four minutes, students write their answers using one color pen or pencil. Encourage students first to answer all the facts they know well and can answer quickly. Then they should go back and use strategies to solve the rest. After four minutes, give students more time to complete the remaining items with the other color pen or pencil.

Using the test results, students should update their new *Multiplication* and *Division Facts I Know* charts.

TIMS Bit

The test follows DPP Item R. It lets you and your students see which multiplication and division facts they still need to study. We recommend 4 minutes for this test.

Students can continue to use the *Triangle Flash Cards* to practice the facts that are not yet circled. Students will continue to practice math facts in the DPP.

Students may include their tests in their portfolios.

Currency

TIMS Task

The currency in the European Union is called a Euro. In 2002, 1 Euro was worth 90 cents in the United States. Make a graph to show the number of Euros and their U.S. value. Graph Number of Euros on the horizontal axis and Value in U.S. Dollars and Cents on the vertical axis.

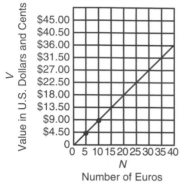

The Value of Euros in U.S. Dollars and Cents

1. How much were 30 Euros worth in U.S. money?

1. $27.00

2. Almost 35 Euros

2. If you trade $30.00 of U.S. money for Euros, about how many Euros will you receive?

Name _____   Date _____

Multiplication and Division Fact Inventory Test

You will need two pens or pencils of different colors. Use the first color when you begin the test. When your teacher tells you to switch pens, finish the test using the second color.

5 × 5 =	24 ÷ 6 =	10 × 7 =	15 ÷ 3 =
8 × 7 =	20 ÷ 10 =	7 × 7 =	10 × 3 =
28 ÷ 4 =	54 ÷ 9 =	36 ÷ 6 =	9 × 5 =
5 × 2 =	20 ÷ 5 =	8 × 8 =	60 ÷ 6 =
4 × 2 =	24 ÷ 8 =	2 × 7 =	10 × 10 =
10 × 9 =	16 ÷ 4 =	9 × 9 =	16 ÷ 2 =
8 × 4 =	42 ÷ 7 =	9 × 4 =	10 × 5 =
3 × 3 =	35 ÷ 7 =	7 × 9 =	48 ÷ 6 =
6 ÷ 3 =	3 × 6 =	27 ÷ 3 =	10 × 4 =
72 ÷ 8 =	6 × 5 =	12 ÷ 4 =	7 × 3 =
18 ÷ 2 =	40 ÷ 8 =	2 × 2 =	80 ÷ 8 =
12 ÷ 6 =			

Lesson 1

Experiment Review

Lesson Overview

Students review the labs they completed during the first seven units by recounting various elements of each lab: variables, number of trials, type of graph, problems solved, and so on. To help them recall each lab, they use their *Student Guides* and work collected in their portfolios. The class discusses the differences and similarities of the experiments.

Key Content

- Comparing and contrasting the following elements of different laboratory investigations:
    - measurement procedures
    - number of trials
    - problems solved
    - types of graphs
    - variables

Key Vocabulary

- bar graph
- point graph
- trial
- variable

Math Facts

Complete DPP Task B, which reviews multiplication and division facts.

Homework

Assign Part 1 of the Home Practice.

Assessment

Use the *Observational Assessment Record* to note students' abilities to organize, graph, and analyze data.

Materials List

Supplies and Copies

Student	Teacher
Supplies for Each Student • student portfolio	**Supplies**
Copies	**Copies/Transparencies** • 1 transparency of *Distance vs. Time Graph* (*Unit Resource Guide* Page 34) • 1 transparency of *Experiment Review Chart* (*Discovery Assignment Book* Pages 135–136) or large sheet of paper for a class chart • 1 copy of *Observational Assessment Record* to be used throughout this unit (*Unit Resource Guide* Pages 11–12)

All blackline masters including assessment, transparency, and DPP masters are also on the Teacher Resource CD.

Student Books
Experiment Review (*Student Guide* Page 270)
Triangle Flash Cards Master (*Discovery Assignment Book* Pages 131–134)
Experiment Review Chart (*Discovery Assignment Book* Pages 135–136)

Daily Practice and Problems and Home Practice
DPP items A–B (*Unit Resource Guide* Pages 15–16)
Home Practice Part 1 (*Discovery Assignment Book* Page 127)

Note: Classrooms whose pacing differs significantly from the suggested pacing of the units should use the Math Facts Calendar in Section 4 of the *Facts Resource Guide* to ensure students receive the complete math facts program.

Assessment Tools
Observational Assessment Record (*Unit Resource Guide* Pages 11–12)

Daily Practice and Problems

Suggestions for using the DPPs are on page 32.

A. Bit: Measuring Area (URG p. 15)

1. Rectangle ABCD has a length of 6 cm and a width of 8 cm. What is its area?

2. Rectangle JKLM is 20 cm by 4.8 cm. How many times greater is its area than rectangle ABCD?

B. Task: Multiplication and Division Facts (URG p. 16)

With a partner, use the *Triangle Flash Cards* to quiz each other on the multiplication facts. Have your partner cover the shaded number (the product). Use the two uncovered numbers to solve a multiplication fact. As you are quizzed, sort the cards into three piles: those facts you know well and can answer quickly, those you know using a strategy, and those you need to learn. Then, circle the facts you know well and can answer quickly on a clean copy of the *Multiplication Facts I Know* chart.

Next, quiz each other on the division facts. To quiz you on the division facts, have your partner cover the numbers in the circles first and then the numbers in the squares. Solve a division fact with the two uncovered numbers. Sort the cards and record your progress on a clean copy of the *Division Facts I Know* chart.

List the facts you have not yet circled on both your charts. Take the flash cards for these facts home so you can practice them. Your teacher will tell you when to expect the test on these facts.

The *Experiment Review* Activity Page in the *Student Guide* provides a context for a class discussion reviewing the labs completed during the year. Professor Peabody is reminded of the lab *Distance vs. Time* from Unit 3 as he times students running the 50-yard dash at a school field day.

During this activity, the class lists the labs they have completed so far this year. Then assign each lab to a group of students for review. Begin the review with a whole-class discussion of the lab *Distance vs. Time* using **Question 2** as a guide. A transparency master of a sample graph for *Distance vs. Time* is provided to help you review the lab.

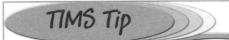

TIMS Tip

If your class did not complete the lab *Distance vs. Time,* use a different lab to begin the discussion.

Question 3 asks students to use their *Student Guides* and portfolios to list all the labs they remember working on during the year. After completing this list, assign each group one or two labs to review using **Question 2** as their guide. The *Experiment Review Chart* Activity Pages in the *Discovery Assignment Book* will help organize students' review information. They can use this chart to compare and contrast the experiments.

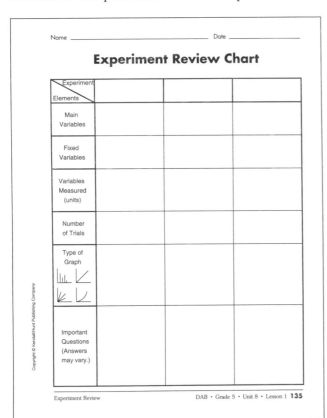

Discovery Assignment Book - page 135 (Answers on p. 35)

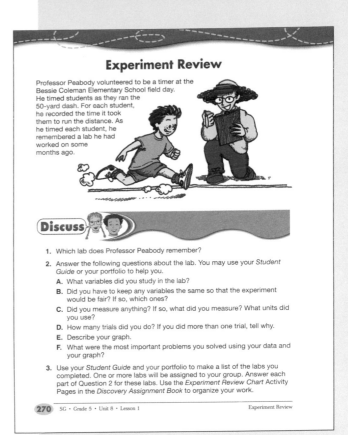

Experiment Review

Professor Peabody volunteered to be a timer at the Bessie Coleman Elementary School field day. He timed students as they ran the 50-yard dash. For each student, he recorded the time it took them to run the distance. As he timed each student, he remembered a lab he had worked on some months ago.

Discuss

1. Which lab does Professor Peabody remember?
2. Answer the following questions about the lab. You may use your *Student Guide* or your portfolio to help you.
    A. What variables did you study in the lab?
    B. Did you have to keep any variables the same so that the experiment would be fair? If so, which ones?
    C. Did you measure anything? If so, what did you measure? What units did you use?
    D. How many trials did you do? If you did more than one trial, tell why.
    E. Describe your graph.
    F. What were the most important problems you solved using your data and your graph?
3. Use your *Student Guide* and your portfolio to make a list of the labs you completed. One or more labs will be assigned to your group. Answer each part of Question 2 for these labs. Use the *Experiment Review Chart* Activity Pages in the *Discovery Assignment Book* to organize your work.

270 SG • Grade 5 • Unit 8 • Lesson 1   Experiment Review

Student Guide - page 270 (Answers on p. 35)

Discovery Assignment Book - page 136 (Answers on p. 36)

After all groups complete their reviews, have each group report to the class. Organize information from all the groups on a class chart using large chart paper or transparencies of the *Experiment Review Chart* Activity Pages, as shown in Figure 1. Note that sample responses to **Question 2** for *Distance vs. Time* are in the third column. Your class answers may vary from the responses here.

Elements \ Experiment	Eyelets	Searching the Forest	Distance vs. Time	Spreading Out	A Day at the Races	Flipping Two Coins
Main Variables	number of eyelets/ number of pairs of shoes	color/number of tiles pulled	distance and time	number of drops/area of spot	time/ distance/ speed	number of heads/ percent of sample
Fixed Variables	definition of eyelets	sample size, rules for setting up bags	pace, timing procedure	size of drop, type of towel, type of liquid, procedure for dropping liquid	timing procedure, distance in 6-yard race, time in 3-second race	procedure for flipping coins, same coins
Variables Measured (units)	none	none	time in seconds, distance in yards	area in sq cm	time in seconds, distance in feet	none
Number of Trials	1	3	3	3	3	10, 100, 1000
Type of Graph						
Important Questions (Answers may vary.)	How many eyelets on all the shoes in the class?	Predict the number of tiles of each color in the bag.	Find the speed that a person walks.	Predict the area of a spot made with a different number of drops.	Compare speeds of students walking, running, etc.	Predict the percent of times heads will come up when flipping two coins many times.

Figure 1: *A sample experiment review class chart*

After all groups report and the information is displayed, continue discussion using the following questions:

- *When doing an experiment, why do you need to keep some variables fixed?* (To be able to look for patterns and make predictions using the main variables in an experiment, other variables must be held fixed. Otherwise, we won't know which variable caused the change in the experimental data. For example, in *Spreading Out,* when students look for the relationship between the number of drops of water and the area of the spot made on a paper towel, it is necessary to use the same brand of paper towels. Otherwise, the size of the drops may vary due to the change in paper towel brand as well as the number of drops.)

- *Why do we often have to do more than one trial when doing an experiment?* (Since experimental and measurement error are often inevitable, scientists use multiple trials so they can average out the error. However, if error is not likely, one trial may suffice.)

- *How are point graphs used to make predictions?* (If the data points lie close to a straight line, you can draw a best-fit line. You can use this line to make predictions using interpolation or extrapolation. You may wish to show an example of interpolation or extrapolation using the transparency of the *Distance vs. Time Graph.*)

- *Name two experiments that are alike. How are they alike? How are they different?* (While answers may vary, possible student responses follow. *Eyelets* and *Searching the Forest* are alike because they both use bar graphs. In *Eyelets,* you can use the graph to find out which number of eyelets is most common or least common. In *Searching the Forest,* you can use the graph to predict the most common or least common color of tile in the bag. *Distance vs. Time* and *A Day at the Races* are similar because they use a line on a graph to find the speed a person travels. In *Distance vs. Time,* each person walks the same distance as he or she is timed. In *A Day at the Races,* each person moves in a different way as he or she is timed. Each person travels for either a specific period of time or a specific distance.)

TIMS Tip

If students did not complete all the labs during the school year, adjust the chart as needed.

Journal Prompt

Which two experiments did you like best? What did you like about each one? How are they alike? How are they different?

Name _____ Date _____

Unit 8 Home Practice

PART 1 *Triangle Flash Cards: All the Facts*

Study for the test on the multiplication and division facts. Take home the flash cards for the facts you need to study.

Ask a family member to choose one flash card at a time. To quiz you on a multiplication fact, he or she should cover the corner containing the highest number. Multiply the two uncovered numbers.

To quiz you on a division fact, your family member can cover one of the smaller numbers. One of the smaller numbers is circled. The other has a square around it. Use the two uncovered numbers to solve a division fact.

Ask your family member to mix up the multiplication and division facts. He or she should sometimes cover the highest number, sometimes cover the circled number, and sometimes cover the number in the square.

Your teacher will tell you when the test on the facts will be given.

PART 2 **Practicing the Operations**

1. Use paper and pencil to solve the following problems. Estimate each answer to make sure it is reasonable. Show your work on a separate sheet of paper.
   A. $72 \times 61 =$ B. $0.43 + 7.6 =$ C. $3804 \div 7 =$ D. $61 \times 0.29 =$

2. Estimate the following answers. Describe your strategy for each.
   A. $78,000 \div 40$

   B. $104,000 \div 27$

   C. 9821×14

   D. $178 \times 324,000$

APPLICATIONS: AN ASSESSMENT UNIT   DAB · Grade 5 · Unit 8 **127**

Discovery Assignment Book - page 127

Math Facts

DPP item B reviews all the multiplication and division facts.

Homework and Practice

- DPP Bit A reviews area.
- Assign Part 1 of the Home Practice, which asks students to use *Triangle Flash Cards* with a family member to review the multiplication and division facts they need to study.

Answers for Part 1 of the Home Practice are in the Answer Key at the end of this lesson and at the end of this unit.

Assessment

Use the *Observational Assessment Record* to note students' abilities to organize, graph, and analyze data.

At a Glance

Math Facts and Daily Practice and Problems

Complete DPP items A–B. Item A reviews area. Task B reviews multiplication and division facts.

Teaching the Activity

1. Read the opening paragraph on the *Experiment Review* Activity Page in the *Student Guide.*
2. Review the lab *Distance vs. Time* using **Question 2** on the *Experiment Review* Activity Page.
3. Students work in groups to review other labs completed throughout the year using their *Student Guides,* portfolios, **Question 2** on the *Experiment Review* Activity Page, and the *Experiment Review Chart* in the *Discovery Assignment Book.*
4. Each group reports its review information to the class, and the class creates a table showing the components of each lab.
5. Using the prompts in the Lesson Guide, lead a class discussion. Students compare and contrast labs to find similarities and differences.

Homework

Assign Part 1 of the Home Practice.

Assessment

Use the *Observational Assessment Record* to note students' abilities to organize, graph, and analyze data.

Answer Key is on pages 35–36.

Notes:

Distance vs. Time Graph

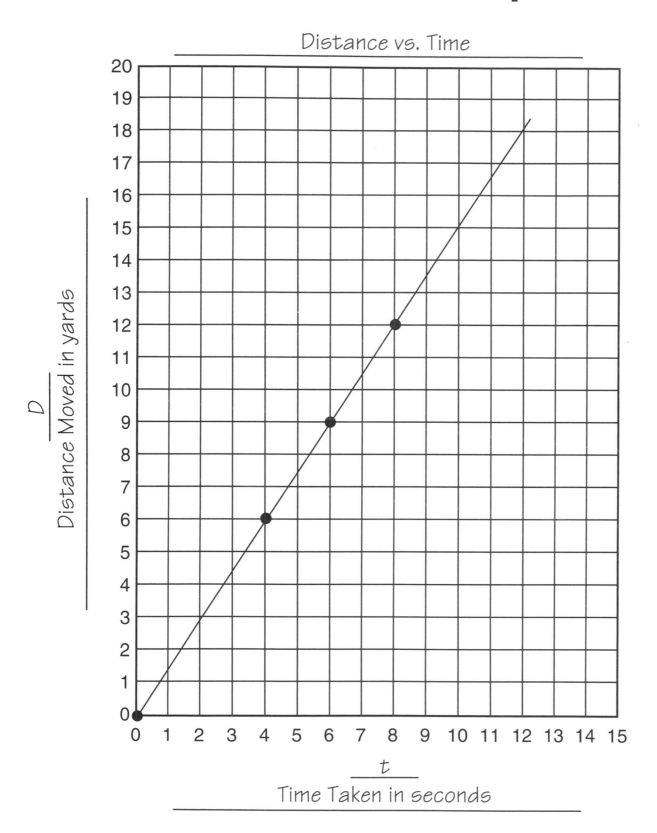

Transparency Master

Student Guide (p. 270)

Experiment Review

1. *Distance vs. Time*

2. **A.** distance, time, and speed

   B. pacing, timing procedure, etc.

   C. Yes, we measured time in seconds and distance in yards.

   D. We did 3 trials to make sure our data was accurate.

   E. The graph is a point graph with a line that starts at (0 seconds, 0 yards) and goes uphill.

   F. We found the speed at which a student walks.

3. See the Experiment Review Chart in Figure 1 in Lesson Guide 1.*

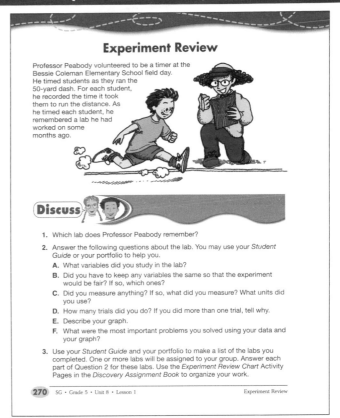

Student Guide - page 270

Discovery Assignment Book (p. 135)

Experiment Review Chart

See Figure 1 in Lesson Guide 1 for a sample table.*

Discovery Assignment Book - page 135

*Answers and/or discussion are included in the Lesson Guide.

Name _____ Date _____			
Experiment Elements			
Main Variables			
Fixed Variables			
Variables Measured (units)			
Number of Trials			
Type of Graph			
Important Questions (Answers may vary.)			

136 DAB • Grade 5 • Unit 8 • Lesson 1   Experiment Review

Discovery Assignment Book - page 136

Discovery Assignment Book (p. 136)

See Figure 1 in Lesson Guide 1 for a sample table.*

*Answers and/or discussion are included in the Lesson Guide.

Optional Lesson 2

Three in a Row

Lesson Overview

Students play a game that estimates the product of decimals.

Key Content

- Estimating products of decimals.
- Using fractions and decimals to represent the same quantity.

Math Facts

Remind students to practice their facts at home using their *Triangle Flash Cards*.

Homework

Have students play the game at home.

Materials List

Supplies and Copies

Student	Teacher
Supplies for Each Student • 8–10 game markers or tokens of one color • calculator	**Supplies**
Copies	**Copies/Transparencies** • 1 transparency of *Three in a Row* game board (*Discovery Assignment Book* Page 139)

All blackline masters including assessment, transparency, and DPP masters are also on the Teacher Resource CD.

Student Books

Three in a Row (*Discovery Assignment Book* Pages 137–139)

Teaching the Activity

Introduce the game by reading the *Three in a Row* Game Pages in the *Discovery Assignment Book*. Demonstrate it by playing with a student on the overhead using a transparency of the game board. To play this game, each student pair needs only one game board from the *Discovery Assignment Book*. A player chooses two factors from the factor frame and finds their product using a calculator. (If they want, players may choose one factor and multiply it by itself: i.e., $4.93 \times 4.93 \approx 25$.) The player then covers the square with the number closest to the product on his or her calculator display. The first student to cover three squares in a row, horizontally, vertically, or diagonally, is the winner.

This is a game of estimation and strategy—students should look for patterns as they multiply the factors they choose. After students play, discuss the strategies they used to choose their factors. You can send this game home or use it in an activity center.

TIMS Tip

For game tokens, students can use two colors of centimeter cubes, two kinds of beans, or small scraps of paper with their initials.

Math Facts

Remind students to practice the multiplication and division facts using their *Triangle Flash Cards*.

Homework and Practice

Students can play the game at home with a family member or friend.

Extension

Students can create their own game boards.

Resource

This game is based on a game entitled *Calculator Game Board: Multiplication* from *Family Math*, written by Jean Kerr Stenmark, Virginia Thompson, and Ruth Cossey. *Family Math* is published by the Lawrence Hall of Science, University of California, Berkeley, California.

Name _____ Date _____

Three in a Row

Players

This is a game for two players.

Materials

- one calculator per player
- 8–10 game markers or tokens of one color or shape for each player
- one factor frame and product board per student pair

Rules

1. Player One selects two factors from the factor frame and finds their product with a calculator. He or she may select two different factors or use the same factor twice.
2. One of the player's markers is placed on the product board on the square with the number that is closest to the product of the two factors.
3. Player Two chooses two factors and follows the same steps described above.
4. Two markers may not occupy the same space.
5. The game continues until one player has three markers in a row, horizontally, vertically, or diagonally.

Three in a Row   DAB • Grade 5 • Unit 8 • Lesson 2 **137**

Discovery Assignment Book - page 137 (Answers on p. 41)

Name _____ Date _____

Game Board

Factor Frame

| 0.493 | 0.109 | 4.93 | 109 | 49.3 | 0.01 | 493 |

Product Board

10	500	2500	5
250	0.05	1	25,000
5000	50,000	25	50
$2\frac{1}{2}$	0.005	$\frac{1}{1000}$	$\frac{1}{2}$

Three in a Row   DAB • Grade 5 • Unit 8 • Lesson 2 **139**

Discovery Assignment Book - page 139 (Answers on p. 41)

Math Facts

Remind students to practice their facts at home using their *Triangle Flash Cards.*

Teaching the Activity

1. Read and review the game's directions on the *Three in a Row* Game Pages in the *Discovery Assignment Book.*
2. Use a transparency of the game board in the *Discovery Assignment Book* to demonstrate the game.
3. Student pairs play the game.
4. After students play the game, discuss strategies students used to choose factors.

Homework

Have students play the game at home.

Extension

Students can create their own game boards.

Answer Key is on page 41.

Notes:

Discovery Assignment Book (pp. 137, 139)

Three in a Row

See Lesson Guide 2 for a discussion of the game.

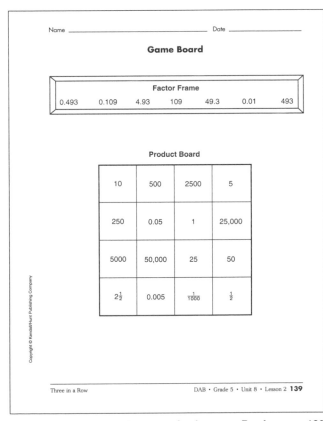

Name _____ Date _____

Three in a Row

Players

This is a game for two players.

Materials

- one calculator per player
- 8–10 game markers or tokens of one color or shape for each player
- one factor frame and product board per student pair

Rules

1. Player One selects two factors from the factor frame and finds their product with a calculator. He or she may select two different factors or use the same factor twice.
2. One of the player's markers is placed on the product board on the square with the number that is closest to the product of the two factors.
3. Player Two chooses two factors and follows the same steps described above.
4. Two markers may not occupy the same space.
5. The game continues until one player has three markers in a row, horizontally, vertically, or diagonally.

Three in a Row   DAB • Grade 5 • Unit 8 • Lesson 2 **137**

Discovery Assignment Book - page 137

Name _____ Date _____

Game Board

Factor Frame

0.493	0.109	4.93	109	49.3	0.01	493

Product Board

10	500	2500	5
250	0.05	1	25,000
5000	50,000	25	50
$2\frac{1}{2}$	0.005	$\frac{1}{1000}$	$\frac{1}{2}$

Three in a Row   DAB • Grade 5 • Unit 8 • Lesson 2 **139**

Discovery Assignment Book - page 139

Lesson 3

Florence Kelley

Lesson Overview

Estimated Class Sessions

1

Part 1 of the lesson is an *Adventure Book* story about Florence Kelley, a prominent social reformer who worked at Hull House in Chicago around 1900. She documented social problems through survey data.

Part 2 of the lesson is a discussion of Florence Kelley's data in the *Student Guide.* The story and discussion provide the context for the open-ended assessment problem in Lesson 4 *Florence Kelley's Report.*

One of the problems Kelley documented in the late 1800s was the employment of young children. The *Adventure Book* begins with a fact-based account of Francesca, a young immigrant girl mentioned in Kelley's survey notes. Francesca takes classes in English at Jane Addams's Hull House where Florence Kelley is the English teacher.

The story shifts to Kelley's work. Horrified by the ill treatment of children in factories and sweatshops, Kelley is determined to prove the extent of the problem by collecting data and writing fact-filled reports for the government. Implicit in the story are the ideas that math and science are powerful tools for measuring social phenomena and that gathering data is the first step in identifying areas that need improvement. Kelley's survey method is described and one of her original data tables is presented as an illustration. The story ends optimistically with Kelley's prediction—based on her data—that the number of children employed in Illinois will decrease.

Key Content

- Connecting math and science to real-world events.
- Organizing and analyzing data.

Key Vocabulary

- immigrant
- settlement house
- sweatshops

Math Facts

DPP item C provides practice with multiplication and division facts using variables in number sentences.

Homework

1. Assign DPP Task D, which practices estimation and operations.
2. Assign Part 5 of the Home Practice, which reviews reading and interpreting data in a bar graph.

Assessment

Use Lesson 4 *Florence Kelley's Report* to assess students' abilities to analyze and display data as well as communicate mathematically.

Materials List

Supplies and Copies

Student	Teacher
Supplies for Each Student • calculator	**Supplies**
Copies	**Copies/Transparencies** • 1 transparency of *Increase in Work Done: Third Annual Report* (*Unit Resource Guide* Page 50)

All blackline masters including assessment, transparency, and DPP masters are also on the Teacher Resource CD.

Student Books

Florence Kelley (*Student Guide* Pages 271–272)
Florence Kelley (*Adventure Book* Pages 47–60)

Daily Practice and Problems and Home Practice

DPP items C–D (*Unit Resource Guide* Page 17)
Home Practice Part 5 (*Discovery Assignment Book* Page 129)

Note: Classrooms whose pacing differs significantly from the suggested pacing of the units should use the Math Facts Calendar in Section 4 of the *Facts Resource Guide* to ensure students receive the complete math facts program.

Daily Practice and Problems

Suggestions for using the DPPs are on page 49.

C. Bit: Fact Practice I (URG p. 17)

Find *n* to make each number sentence true.

A. $5 \times 8 = n$ B. $3 \times n = 21$

C. $36 \div 6 = n$ D. $n \times 5 = 10$

E. $10 \times 4 = n$ F. $20 \div n = 4$

G. $12 \div 3 = n$ H. $9 \times 6 = n$

I. $n \times 8 = 64$

D. Task: Practicing the Operations
(URG p. 17)

Solve the following using paper and pencil. Estimate to make sure your answers are reasonable.

A. $62 \times 48 =$ B. $871 \div 6 =$

C. $36.3 \times 0.5 =$ D. $8243 - 738 =$

E. $21.8 \times 5 =$ F. $8.2 \times .47 =$

G. $76 \times 200 =$ H. $34 \times 800 =$

I. $8294 + 5088 =$

Supreme Court Justice Felix Frankfurter once described Florence Kelley as *"the woman who probably had the largest single share in shaping the social history of the United States during the first thirty years of this century."* While many female reformers of her day organized protests against the government, Kelley chose instead to work with the government in order to effect the passing of legislation in favor of her causes.

Kelley was among the first social scientists to use rigorous survey methods to collect demographic data and among the first to analyze such data and use it in meaningful ways. Her reports to the government were therefore highly effective and influential. Her Illinois factory reports resulted in the passage of laws that prohibited the employment of children under 14 and established the limit of an 8-hour workday for women and children. After seven years at Hull House in Chicago, Florence Kelley moved to New York to help lead the National Consumers League, where she continued to fight poor conditions in factories and sweatshops by organizing consumer boycotts. Kelley was also prominent in women's suffrage and civil rights movements.

Teaching the Activity

Students should read the *Adventure Book* first to enjoy the story. Then use the discussion prompts to discuss the details of the story.

Page 54

• Why did the government want a survey of the neighborhood?

The government wanted to gather precise data on the living and working conditions of the poor. It wanted to know what problems most needed attention. It wanted data it could use later to see whether conditions had improved or worsened.

• *Why was the survey important to Florence Kelley?*

She wanted to convince the public and lawmakers that child employment was a real problem. She understood the power that facts and numbers would give to her arguments for reforms.

Page 55

• *How young were some of the children that Florence Kelley found working?*

She found children as young as three years old working. She saw toddlers pulling basting threads out of clothing. (You may need to define the term basting threads for students.)

Florence Kelley

Jane Addams smiled calmly at her spirited friend. "Ah, then you will be very interested in this letter from the Illinois Bureau of Labor Statistics. They would like you to write a report on the sweatshops of Chicago."

Kelley was immediately interested. "What exactly do they want?" she asked, as she skimmed through the letter.

"It is a huge task," admitted Addams. "They want you to make at least 1000 visits in the neighborhood—go to shops, factories, businesses, and homes and ask the people a long list of questions. That way, the government will be able to gather precise data on what living and working conditions are like for the poor."

Kelley jumped up and began to pace the room. "Yes! This is the kind of research I've been saying should be done! By collecting actual numbers, and by doing it again in future years, we will be able to show whether things are getting better or worse. This is exactly the kind of data that agencies need if they are to plan effective programs to help the poor! Investigating the sweatshops will provide real data to convince the public and the lawmakers that child labor is a real problem."

Addams was not surprised at Kelley's enthusiasm. "I knew you would see the importance of this survey. That was why I recommended you for the job."

"Oh, thank you, Miss Addams!" Kelley exclaimed. "I can't wait to get started!"

In the years that followed, Florence Kelley continued to gather data. Her surveys included factories and households as well as the sweatshops. She and her assistants spent many long days trudging the streets of Chicago. They knocked on doors, wrote down what they saw, and asked people questions.

Adventure Book - page 54

Florence Kelley

They saw homes that were neat and clean and homes that were bare and dirty. Some apartments had no windows. The air inside smelled of coal stoves and cooking grease. Many had no running water or toilets. Some of the factories were even worse, with their loud and dangerous machines. Some people even lived in the same rooms in which they operated small businesses or factories. Here children as young as three years old could be found hard at work beside their parents. Even toddlers could pull the basting threads out of clothing that had been stitched by their mothers.

Adventure Book - page 55

Florence Kelley

Kelley and her workers talked to hundreds of people and asked many questions. They asked how many children were in each family and where the people worked. They found out how much money each family earned and what languages they spoke. They learned where people had been born and whether they could read and write. They took careful notes and kept a record of every answer.

In the course of her investigations, Florence Kelley was able to prove that great numbers of children were working instead of going to school. These children were poor and uneducated and often worked long hours in terrible conditions. By using her survey data to support her arguments, she convinced many more people that there was a serious problem and that something should be done about it.

However, Kelley did not believe that the United States government in Washington, D.C., would be able to change this anytime soon. She decided to ask the Illinois state legislators to investigate for themselves, in the hope that they would pass state laws against child labor. She wrote reports and made speeches. She even took the lawmakers on tours of the worst factories to show them firsthand what children were being exposed to.

56   AB • Grade 5 • Unit 8 • Lesson 3

Adventure Book - page 56

Page 56

- *What variables did Florence Kelley study in her survey? Label each variable as numerical or categorical.*

Number of children in a family. (Numerical)

Where people worked. (Categorical)

How much money families earned. (Numerical)

Languages spoken. (Categorical)

Where people were born. (Categorical)

Number of children who worked. (Numerical)

- *How did Florence Kelley use the information she collected?*

She used the data to convince people there was a serious problem. She wrote reports and made speeches to convince lawmakers to pass laws addressing the problem of child labor.

Florence Kelley

In the summer of 1893, Illinois passed its first factory law. The law made it illegal for children to work more than eight hours a day and illegal for children under the age of fourteen to work at all. There was also a requirement that factories be inspected to make sure they were obeying the new law. Florence Kelley was appointed the first Chief Inspector of Factories in Illinois, a job she energetically carried out for four years.

AB • Grade 5 • Unit 8 • Lesson 3   57

Adventure Book - page 57

Page 57

- *What law did Illinois pass in 1893? What did the law say?*

In 1893, Illinois passed its first factory law. The law made it illegal for children to work more than 8 hours a day and illegal for children under the age of fourteen to work at all. The factories had to be inspected to make sure they were obeying the law. Florence Kelley was the first Chief Factory Inspector of Illinois.

Page 58

- *What did Florence Kelley do as Chief Factory Inspector?*

She wrote a report every year that included all the facts she collected.

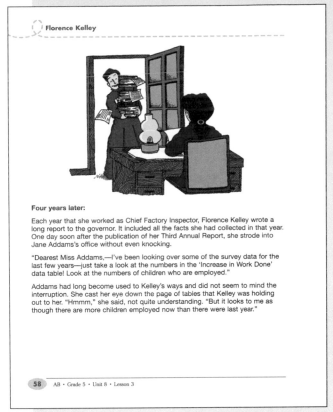

Adventure Book - page 58

Page 60

- *How did the report affect the lawmakers and the factory owners?*

It was important for the lawmakers and for the public to know about problems in the factories. Florence Kelley believed that if people knew about a problem, they would want to solve it. Writing the reports also showed the government that the inspectors were doing the job they were hired to do. Factory owners breaking the law were named in the reports and this bad publicity caused them to lose some customers. To keep their customers happy, owners began to comply with the law.

Adventure Book - page 60

Florence Kelley

Florence Kelley was Chief Inspector of Factories in Illinois. She wrote a report with all the facts she collected during the year. Here is the data table for her third report.

Third Annual Report
of the
Factory Inspectors of Illinois

Increase in Work Done

Year	Places inspected	Men employed	Women employed	Children employed	Total employed
1895............................	4,540	151,075	30,670	8,624	190,369
1894............................	3,440	97,600	24,335	8,130	130,065
Increase.................	1,100	53,475	6,335	494	60,304
1895............................	4,540	151,075	30,670	8,624	190,369
1893............................	2,362	52,480	17,288	6,456	76,224
Increase.................	2,178	98,595	13,382	2,168	114,145

 Discuss

1. Study the data table.
   A. How many children were employed in 1895?
   B. Where did you find this information?
   C. How many children were employed in 1894? 1893?
   D. Was there an increase or decrease in the number of children employed from 1894 to 1895?
   E. Was the number of children employed in 1894 more or less than the number employed in 1893? How many more or less?

2. What do the other columns in the data table tell you?

Florence Kelley   SG • Grade 5 • Unit 8 • Lesson 3   **271**

Student Guide - page 271 (Answers on p. 51)

3. A. How many places were inspected in 1895? 1894? 1893?
   B. Was there an increase or decrease in the number of places inspected from 1894 to 1895?
   C. Was the number of places inspected in 1894 more or less than the number inspected in 1893? How many more or less?

4. In the story, Florence Kelley studies the Third Annual Report and says,

   ". . . I think these numbers show a trend, . . . a trend toward a reduction in the number of children employed. And I predict that because of the new law that this trend will continue."

   A. Do the numbers in the table show a trend toward fewer numbers of children employed? Why or why not?
   B. Was her prediction a good one? Use the data in the table to support your thinking.

272   SG • Grade 5 • Unit 8 • Lesson 3   Florence Kelley

Student Guide - page 272 (Answers on p. 51)

Discussing the Data

Use the questions on the *Florence Kelley* Activity Pages in the *Student Guide* to lead a discussion on the data table in Florence Kelley's third report to the government. (A transparency master of the data is at the end of the Lesson Guide.) The table is a copy of Florence Kelley's actual table in her published report in 1895. *Questions 1–3* familiarize students with the table. Note that the number of children employed in 1895 is listed twice in the table *(Questions 3A–3B)*. Be sure students can locate the number of places inspected and the number of children employed for each year on the table.

Question 4 asks students to interpret the data. In the story Florence Kelley predicts that the number of children employed will decrease. Students must decide, based on the data, if this is a good prediction. If students look carefully at the data, they will see that the number of children employed actually increased each year. However, during the same three years, the number of places inspected also increased each year. Using the data in the table and subtraction, we see that 1674 more children were employed in 1894 (8130 children) than in 1893 (6456 children). However, during the same years 1078 more places were inspected. The table shows that even though 1100 more places were inspected in 1895 than 1894, only 494 more children were employed. Since the increases in the number of children employed are smaller each year even as the number of inspections grows, students can reason that Florence Kelley's prediction is a good one. The trend toward the reduction in the number of children employed will continue.

These questions set the stage for the assessment problem in the next lesson. To complete the assessment, students will be given a data table from Kelley's fourth report in 1896. They will interpret the data and write a report as if they were Kelley.

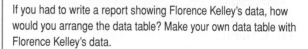

Journal Prompt

If you had to write a report showing Florence Kelley's data, how would you arrange the data table? Make your own data table with Florence Kelley's data.

DPP item C provides practice with multiplication and division facts using variables in number sentences.

- Assign DPP item D, which practices estimation and operations.

- Assign Part 5 of the Home Practice, which reviews reading and interpreting data in a bar graph.

Answers for Part 5 of the Home Practice are in the Answer Key at the end of this lesson and at the end of this unit.

Use Lesson 4 *Florence Kelley's Report* to assess students' abilities to analyze and display data as well as communicate mathematically.

- Addams, Jane. *Twenty Years at Hull-House.* Signet, New York, 1999.

- Goldmark, Josephine. *Impatient Crusader: Florence Kelley's Life Story.* Greenwood Publishing Group, Westport, CT, 1981.

- *Hull-House Maps and Papers.* Ayer Co., New Haven, CT, 1970.

- Sklar, Kathryn Kish. *Florence Kelley and the Nation's Work: The Rise of Women's Political Culture, 1830–1900.* Yale University Press, New Haven, CT, 1995.

- *First Annual Report of the Factory Inspectors of Illinois, for the Year Ending December 15, 1893.* H. W. Rokker, Springfield, IL, 1894.

- *Second Annual Report of the Factory Inspectors of Illinois, for the Year Ending December 15, 1894.* Ed. F. Hartman, Springfield, IL, 1895.

- *Third Annual Report of the Factory Inspectors of Illinois, for the Year Ending December 15, 1895.* Ed. F. Hartman, Springfield, IL, 1896.

- *Fourth Annual Report of the Factory Inspectors of Illinois, for the Year Ending December 15, 1896.* Phillips Bros., Springfield, IL, 1897.

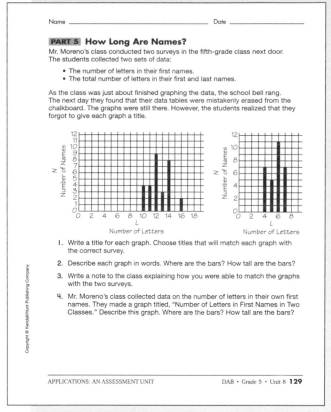

Name _____ Date _____

PART 5 How Long Are Names?

Mr. Moreno's class conducted two surveys in the fifth-grade class next door. The students collected two sets of data:

- The number of letters in their first names.
- The total number of letters in their first and last names.

As the class was just about finished graphing the data, the school bell rang. The next day they found that their data tables were mistakenly erased from the chalkboard. The graphs were still there. However, the students realized that they forgot to give each graph a title.

1. Write a title for each graph. Choose titles that will match each graph with the correct survey.

2. Describe each graph in words. Where are the bars? How tall are the bars?

3. Write a note to the class explaining how you were able to match the graphs with the two surveys.

4. Mr. Moreno's class collected data on the number of letters in their own first names. They made a graph titled, "Number of Letters in First Names in Two Classes." Describe this graph. Where are the bars? How tall are the bars?

APPLICATIONS: AN ASSESSMENT UNIT   DAB • Grade 5 • Unit 8 **129**

Discovery Assignment Book - page 129 (Answers on p. 52)

Increase in Work Done: Third Annual Report

Third Annual Report
of the
Factory Inspectors of Illinois

Increase in Work Done

Year	Places inspected	Men employed	Women employed	Children employed	Total employed
1895..........................	4,540	151,075	30,670	8,624	190,369
1894..........................	3,440	97,600	24,335	8,130	130,065
Increase.................	1,100	53,475	6,335	494	60,304
1895..........................	4,540	151,075	30,670	8,624	190,369
1893..........................	2,362	52,480	17,288	6,456	76,224
Increase.................	2,178	98,595	13,382	2,168	114,145

Transparency Master

Student Guide (p. 271)

Florence Kelley

1. **A.** 8624 children

   B. In the column labeled children employed and in the rows labeled 1895. (Note: The information is in the table twice.)*

   C. 1894: 8130 children; 1893: 6456 children

   D. increase

   E. more; 1674 more children

2. The number of places inspected, the number of men employed, the number of women employed, and the total employed for the years 1893, 1894, and 1895.

Florence Kelley

Florence Kelley was Chief Inspector of Factories in Illinois. She wrote a report with all the facts she collected during the year. Here is the data table for her third report.

**Third Annual Report
of the
Factory Inspectors of Illinois**

Increase in Work Done

Year	Places inspected	Men employed	Women employed	Children employed	Total employed
1895............................	4,540	151,075	30,670	8,624	190,369
1894............................	3,440	97,600	24,335	8,130	130,065
Increase..................	1,100	53,475	6,335	494	60,304
1895............................	4,540	151,075	30,670	8,624	190,369
1893............................	2,362	52,480	17,288	6,456	76,224
Increase..................	2,178	98,595	13,382	2,168	114,145

Discuss

1. Study the data table.
   A. How many children were employed in 1895?
   B. Where did you find this information?
   C. How many children were employed in 1894? 1893?
   D. Was there an increase or decrease in the number of children employed from 1894 to 1895?
   E. Was the number of children employed in 1894 more or less than the number employed in 1893? How many more or less?

2. What do the other columns in the data table tell you?

Florence Kelley   SG • Grade 5 • Unit 8 • Lesson 3   **271**

Student Guide - page 271

Student Guide (p. 272)

3. **A.** 1895: 4540 places; 1894: 3440 places; 1893: 2362 places

   B. increase

   C. more; 1078 places

4.* **A.** Yes, the number of children employed does not increase as fast as the number of places inspected.

   B. Yes, the number of children employed between 1893–1894 increased by 1674 children while the number of places inspected increased by 1078. From 1894 to 1895, while the number of places inspected increased at about the same rate (1100 more places inspected), the number of children employed only increased by 494 children.

3. **A.** How many places were inspected in 1895? 1894? 1893?
   B. Was there an increase or decrease in the number of places inspected from 1894 to 1895?
   C. Was the number of places inspected in 1894 more or less than the number inspected in 1893? How many more or less?

4. In the story, Florence Kelley studies the Third Annual Report and says,

   "...I think these numbers show a trend,...a trend toward a reduction in the number of children employed. And I predict that because of the new law that this trend will continue."

   A. Do the numbers in the table show a trend toward fewer numbers of children employed? Why or why not?
   B. Was her prediction a good one? Use the data in the table to support your thinking.

272 SG • Grade 5 • Unit 8 • Lesson 3   Florence Kelley

Student Guide - page 272

*Answers and/or discussion are included in the Lesson Guide.

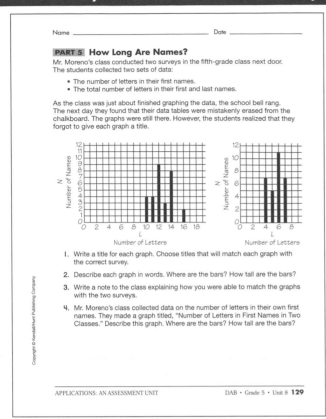

Discovery Assignment Book - page 129

Discovery Assignment Book (p. 129)

Home Practice*

Part 5. How Long Are Names?

1. Answers will vary. The graph on the left can be titled "Number of Letters in First Names" and the graph on the right can be titled "Number of Letters in First and Last Names."

2. Answers will vary. Some students may mention that for the data in the graph on the left there is a larger range for the number of letters (10–16 letters) but shorter bars. The graph on the right has a smaller range for the number of letters (4–7) but more data for the numbers within that range (taller bars).

3. Answers will vary. Students will probably mention that the data for the graph on the left shows a larger number of letters in names than the graph on the right. Therefore, the graph on the left shows the letters for first and last names combined.

4. Answers will vary. Possible response: The bars on the graph will be between 3 and 8 letters. The bars will be about twice as tall as the bars on the graph for one class.

*Answers for all the Home Practice in the *Discovery Assignment Book* are at the end of the unit.

Lesson 4

Florence Kelley's Report

Lesson Overview

Estimated Class Sessions

1-2

The Adventure Book *Florence Kelley* from Lesson 3 provides a context for this assessment. In the book, Florence Kelley collects data on child employment during the years 1893–1895 and publishes the data in a report to the governor. This lesson is an assessment in which students graph and analyze similar data for the years 1893–1896.

Key Content

- Graphing and analyzing data.
- Using data to solve problems.
- Using the Student Rubrics: *Knowing* and *Telling* to self-assess problem-solving skills.
- Solving open-response problems and communicating solution strategies.

Assessment

1. Compare this lesson to work on *Stack Up* in Unit 2.
2. Assess students' abilities to work cooperatively.
3. Use DPP item F to assess students' abilities to communicate mathematically.

Curriculum Sequence

Before This Unit

Analyzing Data

Analysis of data is an integral part of *Math Trailblazers*. Beginning in Unit 1 of fifth grade, students analyzed their own data in Lesson 1 in the lab *Eyelets*, and they analyzed bar graphs in Lesson 3 *Analyzing Data*. They used the Student Rubric: *Knowing* for the first time in fifth grade to guide them as they completed the lab *Searching the Forest* in Lesson 5. They continued to analyze data in labs in Units 2, 3, 4, and 7.

Communicating Mathematically

Throughout the curriculum, questions in activities and labs encourage students to communicate their thinking. To help them communicate mathematically, they were introduced to the Student Rubric: *Telling* in Grade 3 and used it extensively in Grade 4. They used the *Telling* rubric for the first time in fifth grade to help them write their problem-solving strategies in the assessment problem *Stack Up* in Unit 2 Lesson 9.

After This Unit

Analyzing Data

Students will continue to collect and analyze data in labs in Units 13, 14, and 16.

Communicating Mathematically

Throughout the remaining units, students will explain their thinking either in class discussion or in writing. In particular, they will write about their problem-solving strategies in assessment lessons in Units 9, 11, and 16.

Materials List

Supplies and Copies

Student	Teacher
Supplies for Each Student • calculator	**Supplies**
Copies • 1 copy of *Florence Kelley's Report* per student (*Unit Resource Guide* Page 66) • 1–2 copies of *Centimeter Graph Paper* per student (*Unit Resource Guide* Page 67)	**Copies/Transparencies** • 1 copy of *TIMS Multidimensional Rubric* (*Teacher Implementation Guide,* Assessment section) • 1 transparency or poster of Student Rubric: *Knowing* and Student Rubric: *Telling* (*Teacher Implementation Guide,* Assessment section)

All blackline masters including assessment, transparency, and DPP masters are also on the Teacher Resource CD.

Student Books

Student Rubric: *Knowing* (*Student Guide* Appendix A and Inside Back Cover)
Student Rubric: *Telling* (*Student Guide* Appendix C and Inside Back Cover)

Daily Practice and Problems and Home Practice

DPP items E–F (*Unit Resource Guide* Pages 17–18)

Note: Classrooms whose pacing differs significantly from the suggested pacing of the units should use the Math Facts Calendar in Section 4 of the *Facts Resource Guide* to ensure students receive the complete math facts program.

Assessment Tools

TIMS Multidimensional Rubric (*Teacher Implementation Guide,* Assessment section)

Daily Practice and Problems

Suggestions for using the DPPs are on page 64.

E. Bit: Equivalent Fractions (URG p. 17)

Find the equivalent fractions.

A. $\frac{3}{5} = \frac{?}{10}$ B. $\frac{3}{4} = \frac{?}{12}$

C. $\frac{2}{5} = \frac{8}{?}$ D. $\frac{5}{10} = \frac{?}{2}$

E. $\frac{10}{12} = \frac{5}{?}$ F. $\frac{1}{3} = \frac{?}{12}$

G. $\frac{5}{9} = \frac{?}{36}$ H. $\frac{7}{10} = \frac{?}{100}$

F. Challenge: Wall Painting
(URG p. 18)

Michael's family painted the living room and dining room walls. Michael painted $\frac{1}{8}$ of the walls. His sister painted $\frac{1}{4}$ of the walls. Dad painted $\frac{3}{8}$ of the walls. Mom finished the project.

Write three math questions you can ask about Michael's family project. Exchange your problems with a partner or present them to the class to solve.

To prepare for this assessment, students read the Adventure Book *Florence Kelley* in Lesson 3 and discussed the data she collected using the questions on the *Florence Kelley* Activity Pages in the *Student Guide.*

Teaching the Activity

Part 1 Writing the Report

Use the discussion prompts below to review the *Adventure Book.*

- *How did Florence Kelley convince people that child labor was a serious problem?* (She conducted surveys on the living and working conditions of people in Illinois.)

- *Illinois passed its first factory law in 1893. What did the law say about children working in factories?* (Children could not work more than eight hours each day. It was illegal for children under fourteen to work at all.)

- *What was Florence Kelley's job as Chief Factory Inspector?* (She helped inspect the factories and wrote a report to the governor using her data.)

Distribute graph paper and one copy of *Florence Kelley's Report* Assessment Page to each student. Remind students that in the previous lesson they studied the data Florence Kelley included in her Third Annual Report to the governor in 1895. Explain to students that the data table on the assessment page is the one she included in her fourth report for the years 1893–1896.

Encourage students to use the Student Rubrics: *Knowing* and *Telling* to guide their work. Highlight sections of the rubrics that particularly apply to the problem. For example, use the *Telling* rubric to remind students to tell what each number refers to (i.e., 2362 factories or 6456 children). Encourage them to explain how the graphs and number sentences help tell the story of the data. Use the *Knowing* rubric to encourage them to show the mathematical ideas in the report in more than one way, including a graph and words. Point out that you expect a correct graph with a title, appropriate scales, and carefully labeled axes.

TIMS Tip

Students can work on this assessment in several ways. They can complete the assignment individually or with a partner. Alternatively, partners can discuss the data and decide how to set up their graphs and then each student can write his or her report individually.

You may need to help some students get started. Note those students who need help and include that information in your evaluation of their work. Use prompts similar to the following:

- *How many children are employed in each year?*
- *What year are the most children employed?*
- *How many places are inspected each year?*
- *Does the data in the table show that the factory law is working?*
- *How can you use a graph to help explain the data in the table?*

Part 2 Scoring Students' Work

After students draw their graphs and write their reports, give them an opportunity to revise their work based on your comments. Refer to the student rubrics as needed. For example, you may need to remind students to title their graphs or to tell what each number in the report stands for. Remind students to use their graph as a tool for describing the data and showing the trends in child employment.

You can use the Knowing and Telling dimensions of the *TIMS Multidimensional Rubric* to score students' work. See the Assessment section in the *Teacher Implementation Guide* for more information on using the rubric to evaluate students' writing.

To assist you in scoring students' work, questions specific to the task for these dimensions are listed below.

Knowing

- Does the student understand the task? Does he or she use the data in the table to show how the number of children employed changed during the years the law was in effect?
- Can he or she translate between the situation as described in the story, the data table, words, and graphs?
- Did the student draw a graph correctly? Interpret the data correctly?
- Is the student able to track the increases and decreases in the data?
- If applicable, did the student subtract correctly?

Telling

- Is the written response complete and clear?
- Are the arguments logical? Do they follow from the data in the table?
- Does the student refer to the graph in the report, using it to help explain the data?

Content Note

Bar Graph or Point Graph? Either bar graphs or point graphs are appropriate to display this data. Bars are typically used when there are no values in between the data points. A bar graph is appropriate here since there are no years between 1893 and 1894, between 1894 and 1895, etc.

Point graphs are used when there are values between the data points. We can argue that there are values between the years, since there are many days and months between 1894 and 1895. Therefore, plotting points makes sense. If the points form a pattern, we fit a curve or a line to the points to emphasize the patterns in the data.

Three samples of student work follow. Each has been scored using the Knowing and Telling dimensions of the *TIMS Multidimensional Rubric*.

Student A's report.

Florence Kelley

My report is about Florence Kelley and the difference between 1893 and 1896. In 1893 6,456 where working (that is not a lot of people working) In 1894 more people started working, it was up in the 8 thousands. As time went by more people started working in 1895, about 8,624 are now working in 1895. Now in 1896 it got lower to 7,340 people working, that is 1,284 less. (8,624 - -7340=1,284) The places inspected doesn't have glot of jobs for people, but the amount of people is going up witch means there is not alot of places for people work, so they don't have much money and know place to live. So hopefully people came start building places to work.

Student A's graph.

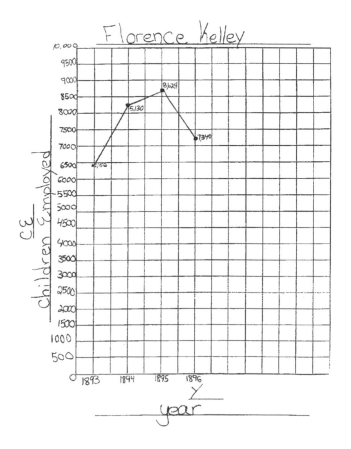

Scoring Student A's work.

Knowing	Level 4	Level 3	Level 2	Level 1
Understands the task's mathematical concepts, their properties and applications…	Completely	Nearly completely	Par~~ti~~ally	Not at all
Translates between words, pictures, symbols, tables, graphs, and real situations…	Readily and without errors	With minor errors	With ma~~jo~~r errors	Not at all
Uses tools (measuring devices, graphs, tables, calculators, etc.) and procedures…	Correctly and efficiently	Correctly or with minor errors	~~Incorrectly~~	Not at all
Uses knowledge of the facts of mathematics (geometry definitions, math facts, etc.)…	Co~~rre~~ctly	With minor errors	With major errors	Not at all

(Level 2 is circled)

Telling	Level 4	Level 3	Level 2	Level 1
Includes response with an explanation and/or description which is…	Complete and clear	Fairly complete and clear	Perhaps ambiguous or unclear	~~Totally unclear or irrelevant~~
Presents supporting arguments which are…	Strong and sound	Logically sound, but may contain minor gaps	Inco~~mple~~te or logica~~lly~~ unsound	Not present
Uses pictures, symbols, tables, and graphs which are…	Correct and clearly relevant	Present with minor errors or some-what irrelevant	Present with errors and/or (irrelevant)	Not present or completely inappropriate
Uses terminology…	Clearly and precisely	With ~~minor errors~~	With major errors	Not at all

(Level 2 is circled; "irrelevant" is circled)

Figure 2: *Student A's work and scores on the rubrics*

Knowing—2

Student A had only a partial understanding of the task. She never mentions child employment. However, she knew to compare the numbers in the Children Employed column. She correctly tracked the increases and decreases in these numbers, using subtraction to show the decrease from 1895 to 1896. She translated the data from the table to the graph correctly, but she shows little understanding of what the numbers mean. For example, her interpretation of the data in the Places Inspected column is very confusing.

Telling—2

Student A had a lot of trouble communicating her thinking. When she uses the number of children employed for each year, she refers instead to people working. Her arguments are illogical and, although her graph is correct, it is not relevant to her discussion of the data.

Student B's report.

Dear Goverment,
I learned what Florence Kelly wanted to happen to the children employed in math. She wanted for less children employed. Florence Kelly got what she wanted but the numbers I'm about to show might look like it is getter bigger but it's not I'll explain. From 1893–1896 for children employed From 1893 there were 6456 and from 1894 there was 8130 also for 1895 and 1896 there were more children employed. But good because there more places inspected each year. I'm glad because there is a deacrease in children employed. Through 1895 and 1896 there was a decrease of 1284 children employed

Student B's graph.

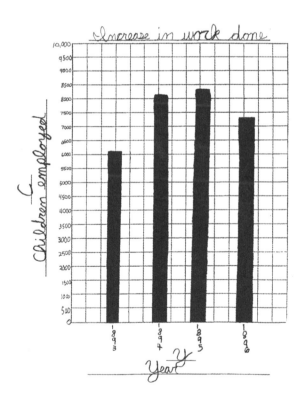

Scoring Student B's work.

Knowing	Level 4	Level 3	Level 2	Level 1
Understands the task's mathematical concepts, their properties and applications…	Com̶pletely	Nearly completely	Partially	Not at all
Translates between words, pictures, symbols, tables, graphs, and real situations…	Readily and without errors	With mi̶nor errors	With major errors	Not at all
Uses tools (measuring devices, graphs, tables, calculators, etc.) and procedures…	Correctly and efficiently	Correctly or with minor er̶rors	Incorrectly	Not at all
Uses knowledge of the facts of mathematics (geometry definitions, math facts, etc.)…	Correctly	With mi̶nor errors	With major errors	Not at all

Telling	Level 4	Level 3	Level 2	Level 1
Includes response with an explanation and/or description which is…	Complete and clear	Fairly complete and clear	Perhaps ambiguous or unclear	Totally unclear or irrelevant
Presents supporting arguments which are…	Strong and sound	Logically sound, but may contain minor gaps	Incomplete or logically unsound	Not present
Uses pictures, symbols, tables, and graphs which are…	Correct and clearly relevant	Present with minor errors or somewhat irrelevant	Present with errors and/or irrelevant	Not present or completely inappropriate
Uses terminology…	Clearly and precisely	With minor errors	With major errors	Not at all

Figure 3: *Student B's work and scores on the rubrics*

Knowing—3

Student B clearly understood the task. He analyzed the child employment data in relation to the number of factories inspected to determine if the numbers of children employed decreased as Florence Kelley predicted in the story. He made connections between the data table, the real situation, and words with few errors. (At one point he says, "for 1895 and 1896 there were more children employed" which is not true. However, he corrects himself in the last line.) He was also able to translate the data into a graph with minor errors.

Telling—3

Student B's response is fairly complete and clear. We can follow his logic, although there are minor gaps, including two statements which are inconsistent. The sentences with child employment data are unclear because he does not label the numbers with "children employed." However, he is able to support his argument, that it ". . . might look like from 1893–1896 for children employment it is getting bigger but its not" with "because there were more places inspected each year." He includes a graph, but it seems to be irrelevant to his conclusions, since he never mentions it in his writing.

Student C's report.

I think the law is working because as I inspected sweat shops, I saw less children working. I saw looking at my graphs that less children were employed and more places were inspected. It looked something like this.

Places Inspected

Children Employed

Student C's graphs.

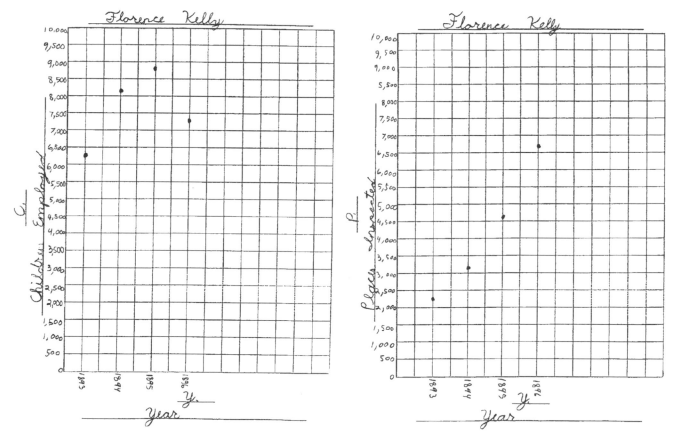

Scoring Student C's work.

Knowing	Level 4	Level 3	Level 2	Level 1
Understands the task's mathematical concepts, their properties and applications…	Com~~pletely~~	Nearly completely	Partially	Not at all
Translates between words, pictures, symbols, tables, graphs, and real situations…	(Readily and without errors)	(With minor errors)	With major errors	Not at all
Uses tools (measuring devices, graphs, tables, calculators, etc.) and procedures…	Correctly and efficiently	Correctly or with minor errors	Incorrectly	Not at all
Uses knowledge of the facts of mathematics (geometry definitions, math facts, etc.)… **N/A**	Correctly	With minor errors	With major errors	Not at all

Telling	Level 4	Level 3	Level 2	Level 1
Includes response with an explanation and/or description which is…	Complete and clear	Fairly complete and clear	Perhaps ambiguous or unclear	Totally unclear or irrelevant
Presents supporting arguments which are…	Strong and sound	(Logically sound, but may contain minor gaps)	(Incomplete or logically unsound)	Not present
Uses pictures, symbols, tables, and graphs which are…	(Correct and clearly relevant)	(Present with minor errors) or somewhat irrelevant	Present with errors and/or irrelevant	Not present or completely inappropriate
Uses terminology… **N/A**	Clearly and precisely	With minor errors	With major errors	Not at all

Figure 4: *Student C's work and scores on the rubrics*

Knowing—3

Student C understood that she needed to analyze the data in both the Places Inspected column and the Children Employed column to see if the factory law was effective. Although there was a minor error in one graph (one point is plotted incorrectly), she translated the real situation from the table to graphs to words.

Telling—3

Student C's explanation is fairly complete and clear, although she does not refer to any numbers in her analysis. She supports her argument that "less children were employed and more places were inspected" by referring to her graphs.

Remind students to practice their math facts using their *Triangle Flash Cards*.

Assessment

- If students include this assessment in their portfolios, they can compare their work on this lesson to their writing for earlier assessment lessons such as *Stack Up* in Unit 2 Lesson 9.

- Use this lesson as an assessment of students' abilities to work together as a group. Tell students they must help Florence Kelley present the data to the state legislature. Groups can plan and present their reports to the whole class.

- Use DPP Challenge F to assess students' abilities to communicate mathematically as they write math problems and present them to their partner or the class. Evaluate students' abilities to express their solution strategies to classmates' math problems.

At a Glance

Math Facts and Daily Practice and Problems

Complete DPP items E–F which include work with fractions.

Before the Activity

Read and discuss the Adventure Book *Florence Kelley* in Lesson 3.

Part 1. Writing the Report

1. Review the Adventure Book using the discussion prompts in Part 1 of this Lesson Guide.
2. Distribute graph paper and the *Florence Kelley's Report* Assessment Page from the *Unit Resource Guide* to students. Calculators should be available.
3. Review the Student Rubrics: *Knowing* and *Telling*. Encourage students to use them as a guide as they work.
4. Students write their reports.

Part 2. Scoring Students' Work

1. Give students a chance to revise their work based on your comments.
2. Score students' reports using the Knowing and Telling dimensions of the *TIMS Multidimensional Rubric*.
3. Students place their completed assessments in their collection folders.

Assessment

1. Compare this lesson to work on *Stack Up* in Unit 2.
2. Assess students' abilities to work cooperatively.
3. Use DPP item F to assess students' abilities to communicate mathematically.

Answer Key is on page 68.

Notes:

Florence Kelley's Report

Imagine that you are Florence Kelley. It has been four years since the factory law was passed in 1893. As part of your job as Chief Factory Inspector, you must write a report to the governor. Here is the data table for your Fourth Annual Report.

Fourth Annual Report
of the
Factory Inspectors of Illinois

Increase in Work Done
1893–1896

Year	Places inspected	Men employed	Women employed	Children employed	Total employed
1896....................	6,707	162,019	30,781	7,340	200,140
1893....................	2,362	52,480	17,288	6,456	76,224
Increase...............	4,345	109,539	13,493	884	123,916
Decrease..............					
1896....................	6,707	162,019	30,781	7,340	200,140
1894....................	3,440	97,600	24,335	8,130	130,065
Increase...............	3,267	64,419	6,446		70,075
Decrease..............				790	
1896....................	6,707	162,019	30,781	7,340	200,140
1895....................	4,540	151,075	30,670	8,624	190,369
Increase...............	2,167	10,944	111		9,771
Decrease..............				1,284	

Use the data in the table to write a report on child employment from 1893 to 1896. Use at least one graph in your report to help you explain the data.

You may use any tools you use in your math class to help you prepare your report. Use the *Knowing* and *Telling* rubrics to guide your work. Write your report on a separate sheet of paper.

Name _____ Date _____

Centimeter Graph Paper, Blackline Master

Name _____ Date _____

Florence Kelley's Report

Imagine that you are Florence Kelley. It has been four years since the factory law was passed in 1893. As part of your job as Chief Factory Inspector, you must write a report to the governor. Here is the data table for your Fourth Annual Report.

Fourth Annual Report
of the
Factory Inspectors of Illinois

Increase in Work Done
1893–1896

Year	Places inspected	Men employed	Women employed	Children employed	Total employed
1896...........................	6,707	162,019	30,781	7,340	200,140
1893...........................	2,362	52,480	17,288	6,456	76,224
Increase.................	4,345	109,539	13,493	884	123,916
Decrease...............					
1896........................	6,707	162,019	30,781	7,340	200,140
1894...........................	3,440	97,600	24,335	8,130	130,065
Increase.................	3,267	64,419	6,446		70,075
Decrease...............				790	
1896........................	6,707	162,019	30,781	7,340	200,140
1895...........................	4,540	151,075	30,670	8,624	190,369
Increase.................	2,167	10,944	111		9,771
Decrease...............				1,284	

Use the data in the table to write a report on child employment from 1893 to 1896. Use at least one graph in your report to help you explain the data.

You may use any tools you use in your math class to help you prepare your report. Use the *Knowing* and *Telling* rubrics to guide your work. Write your report on a separate sheet of paper.

Assessment Blackline Master

Unit Resource Guide - page 66

Unit Resource Guide (p. 66)

Florence Kelley's Report

See Lesson Guide 4 for samples of student work.

Lesson 5

Life Spans

Lesson Overview

Estimated Class Sessions 1-2

Students compare human life span data from 1858 to life span data from 1997. Students are introduced to grouping data into bins or equal intervals. They graph the data and use the graphs to tell the story of the data. This activity prepares students for the assessment lab *Comparing Lives of Animals and Soap Bubbles* in Lesson 6.

Key Content

- Using fractions, decimals, and percents to represent the same quantity.
- Grouping data in bins to see patterns.
- Making and interpreting bar graphs using binned data.
- Translating between graphs and real-world events.
- Connecting mathematics and science to real-world situations.
- Averaging: finding the median.

Key Vocabulary

- binning data

Homework

1. For homework, students can complete the data table and graph for 1997 data. They find the median age at death for this data. *(Questions 9–12)*
2. Assign Part 2 of the Home Practice.

Curriculum Sequence

Before This Unit

Binning and Analyzing Data

Students have analyzed data throughout the curriculum. In Grade 4 Unit 13 students collected data on the number of hours students watched TV, binned the data, and graphed it in a bar graph to analyze it. In Unit 1 Lesson 3 of fifth grade, *Analyzing Data*, they compared three sets of data using bar graphs and analyzed their own data in the labs *Eyelets* in Lesson 1 and *Searching the Forest* in Lesson 5. In Unit 7 Lesson 9 students used bar graphs to display the data in the probability experiment *Flipping Two Coins*.

Fractions, Decimals, and Percents

Students translated between fractions, decimals, and percents in Unit 7. They used percents to compare sets of data in Lesson 1 *Fractions, Decimals, and Percents* and Lesson 9 *Flipping Two Coins*.

After This Unit

Analyzing Data

Students will continue to analyze data throughout the year using different kinds of graphs. In Unit 14 students will analyze and display data in circle graphs.

Fractions, Decimals, and Percents

Fractions, decimals, and percents are used to build circle graphs in Unit 14.

Materials List

Supplies and Copies

Student	Teacher
Supplies for Each Student • calculator	**Supplies**
Copies • 2 copies of *Centimeter Graph Paper* per student (*Unit Resource Guide* Page 67)	**Copies/Transparencies** • 1 transparency of *Graphing Life Spans*, optional (*Unit Resource Guide* Page 80) • 1 transparency of *Life Spans Data Tables*, optional (*Discovery Assignment Book* Page 141)

All blackline masters including assessment, transparency, and DPP masters are also on the Teacher Resource CD.

Student Books
Life Spans (*Student Guide* Pages 273–275)
Life Spans Data Tables (*Discovery Assignment Book* Page 141)

Daily Practice and Problems and Home Practice
DPP items G–H (*Unit Resource Guide* Pages 18–19)
Home Practice Part 2 (*Discovery Assignment Book* Page 127)

Note: Classrooms whose pacing differs significantly from the suggested pacing of the units should use the Math Facts Calendar in Section 4 of the *Facts Resource Guide* to ensure students receive the complete math facts program.

Daily Practice and Problems

Suggestions for using the DPPs are on page 78.

G. Bit: Quick Change (URG p. 18)

Change the following fractions to decimals and then to percents.

A. $\frac{23}{100}$

B. $\frac{3}{4}$

C. $\frac{30}{50}$

D. $\frac{68}{100}$

E. $\frac{5}{10}$

F. $\frac{2}{8}$

G. $\frac{9}{100}$

H. $\frac{2}{40}$

H. Task: Slab-Maker Problem
(URG p. 19)

You need a protractor and centimeter ruler to complete this task. Follow the instructions below to create quadrilateral CDEF.

Make side DE 5 cm long.

Make ∠D 95°.

Make side CD 7 cm long.

Make side EF 3 centimeters shorter than side CD.

Before the Activity

Students will use fractions, decimals, and percents during this activity. Use DPP item G to review translating fractions to decimals to percents.

Teaching the Activity

Part 1 Life Spans

Read the vignette on the *Life Spans* Activity Pages in the *Student Guide*. Discuss the information that David and Brandon gathered at the library, beginning with **Question 1**. Students can see that the ages at death listed in the 1858 data range from infancy to 79 years and the life spans in the 1997 data range from 15 to 97 years.

> ### TIMS Tip
>
> To discourage students from writing in their *Student Guides*, suggest they write both the data sets on their own paper. If they work in pairs, one partner can read the numbers while the other writes them down. Then, as you discuss the data, students can check off numbers as needed.

Students may find it difficult to find trends in the data as it is listed in the *Student Guide*. **Question 2** suggests graphing the data as a way to tell its story. It also asks how to set up the graphs. Students may have many suggestions. Help students evaluate the different methods by asking if the graph they propose will help them "tell the story of the data." That is, will the graph help them see the changes in the length of the life spans in the two sets of data?

To make a useful graph, they need an intermediate step. They can reorganize the data in a table in which they tally the number of deaths at each age. Also, they should group the data into intervals to help illustrate patterns in the data. Use these prompts to guide the discussion:

- *What do we want to compare?* (Life spans—how long people lived—in the mid-1800s to life spans in the late 1900s. Did people live longer in the twentieth century?)

- *What data do we need to make this comparison?* (We need to know how many people in each data set lived to each age. For example, how many people lived to be 60? How many lived to be 50?)

- *How can we find this data?* (Make a new table and tally the number of deaths at each age.)

Life Spans

The students in Mr. Moreno's classroom are studying the history of the United States. They learned that the United States changed rapidly during the 1900s. During this time, many people began working in factories instead of on farms. Living conditions and sanitation improved for most people. At the same time, the discovery of antibiotics and other improvements in medical care changed the way doctors treated diseases.

The students wondered if these changes had any effect on the length of time people lived. Mr. Moreno suggested that they collect information on the life spans of people before these changes occurred. They could then compare them with the life spans of people after these changes occurred. The students decided to compare the life spans of a set of people who lived during the 1800s to the life spans of a set of people who lived during the 1900s.

Brandon and David went to the library to collect data. Brandon looked for obituaries in old newspapers. He looked through newspapers from the year 1858 and found 25 death notices that listed the names of the people who died and their age at death. He wrote down the age of each person: 56 yr, 1 yr 3 mo, 54 yr, 9 mo, 27 yr, 42 yr, 2½ mo, 5 yr, 38 yr, 34 yr, 79 yr, 59 yr, 76 yr, infant, 21 yr, 25 yr, 24 yr, 19 yr, 30 yr, 62 yr, 51 yr, 43 yr, 20 yr, 1 yr, and 5 yr.

David looked in more recent newspapers. He found 50 obituaries that gave the age at death. He wrote down these ages, which were all given in years: 75, 88, 84, 79, 85, 86, 51, 77, 85, 88, 88, 71, 84, 85, 89, 92, 77, 97, 80, 60, 95, 62, 85, 64, 44, 74, 62, 87, 81, 73, 89, 15, 96, 84, 72, 89, 84, 90, 88, 50, 68, 72, 75, 63, 90, 65, 38, 77, 79, and 73. All the people in David's data set died in February of 2007.

 **Discuss**

David and Brandon shared their data with the class.

1. Compare the two sets of life spans. What do you notice about the length of the life spans in the 1858 data and in the 2007 data?

Life Spans   SG • Grade 5 • Unit 8 • Lesson 5   **273**

Student Guide - page 273 (Answers on p. 81)

Content Note

Binning Data. When there are many values and a wide range of values in a data set, it is often impractical to display the data using a bar graph without grouping the data into intervals or **bins.** For example, suppose a principal of a large school collects data on the number of miles teachers drive to school. He finds that the number of miles teachers drive ranges from 1 to 50 miles and no two teachers drive the same number of miles to school. It is not useful to make a bar graph with a scale of 1 to 50 miles on the horizontal axis and one bar for each different number of miles driven. The horizontal axis would be too long and all the bars would be the same height. It is better to group the data into equal intervals or, as we say, to "bin" the data. In this case, the data can be divided into intervals such as 0–9 miles, 10–19 miles, 20–29 miles, etc. Then a bar can be drawn for each interval. Note: The bars are drawn between the lines to show that the data lie within the interval. For example, the first bar tells us that ten teachers drive between 0 and 9 miles to work.

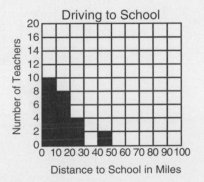

Student Guide - page 274 (Answers on p. 81)

TIMS Tip

The intervals or bins should not overlap and should be the same size. For example, students should not choose intervals from 0–10 years, 10–20 years, or 20–30 years. Using these bins, students will not know where to tally life spans of 10, 20, or 30 years. Choosing the last bin to be "over 60 years" is also problematic, since this bin is larger than the others.

• *How would you graph this data? What variable would you put on the horizontal axis? What variable would you put on the vertical axis?* (Put the age in years on the horizontal axis and the number of deaths at each age on the vertical axis.)

• *If you made a bar graph of the 1858 data, how would you need to scale the horizontal axis? Is this practical?* (From 0 to 79. No, this scale is not practical since the scale won't fit on the graph paper.)

• *How tall would most of the bars be?* (Most of the bars would be very small. Since they would all be about the same height, they would not give much information. Figure 5 shows what the beginning of a bar graph would look like with the horizontal axis scaled by ones.)

You can suggest to students that they need a new way to organize the data to help them see trends in the data. In the *Student Guide,* Mr. Moreno suggests that students bin the data. Explain that you bin data so it will be easier to graph and to see patterns in the data better. Ask students to look at the life span data and suggest possible intervals to use *(Question 3).* One suggestion is to use intervals of 10 years. Intervals will then be 0–9 years, 10–19 years, 20–29 years, 30–39 years, and so on until there are bins for all data.

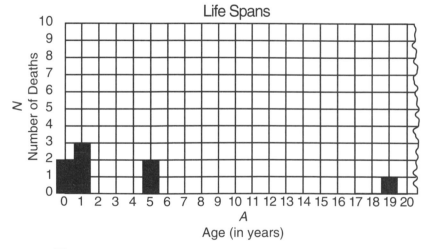

Figure 5: *Scaling the horizontal axis by ones is impractical.*

Question 4 asks students how they can compare data if their samples are different sizes. There are 25 life spans in the 1858 data and 50 life spans in the 1997 data. Students had some experience with this in Unit 7. Remind students that when Lee Yah and her cousin compared data from their class survey on favorite sports (Unit 7 Lesson 1), they found they could more easily compare the data using decimals and percents. Remind students that when you use percents, one whole equals 100. Therefore, when you convert to percents, you show what part, out of 100, of your sample you are considering. This allows you to compare samples of different sizes accurately.

Part 2 Graphing Life Spans Data

Students can use the blank data tables on the *Life Spans Data Tables* Activity Page in the *Discovery Assignment Book* to bin their data *(Question 5)*. Figure 6 shows a sample table. Note that intervals are the same size and do not overlap.

Remind students that the number of tallies in the 1858 data table should equal 25 and the sum of the percents should equal 100%.

After completing the table, *Question 6* asks students to graph the data using a bar graph. However, this graph will be somewhat different from other bar

1858 Data Table

A Age (in years)	N Number of Deaths		Fraction of Deaths	Percent of Deaths (to the Nearest Percent)
	Tallies	Number		
0–9	⊬⊬ II	7	$\frac{7}{25}$	28%
10–19	I	1	$\frac{1}{25}$	4%
20–29	⊬⊬	5	$\frac{5}{25}$	20%
30–39	III	3	$\frac{3}{25}$	12%
40–49	II	2	$\frac{2}{25}$	8%
50–59	IIII	4	$\frac{4}{25}$	16%
60–69	I	1	$\frac{1}{25}$	4%
70–79	II	2	$\frac{2}{25}$	8%
80–89		0	$\frac{0}{25}$	0%
90–99		0	$\frac{0}{25}$	0%

Figure 6: *1858 data table*

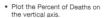

- Plot the Percent of Deaths on the vertical axis.
- Plot the Age in Years on the horizontal axis.
- Draw the bars between the lines to show that most of the ages fall between the numbers on the horizontal axis.
- When you start graphing the data, your graph might look like the graph to the right.

7. Describe the shape of your graph. The shape of the graph tells the story of the data. Use these questions to help you.
   - Are all the bars about the same height, or are some bars much taller than others?
   - Where are the tallest bars—at the beginning, middle, or end of the graph?
   - What do the heights of the bars tell you about life spans in this set of data?

8. **A.** Use your graph to estimate the median life span for the 1858 data.
   B. Use your data to find the median life span.

9. Use the 2007 data to complete a data table like the one in Question 5.

10. Make a bar graph of the 2007 data.
    - Plot the Age in Years on the horizontal axis and the Percent of Deaths on the vertical axis.
    - Use the same scales you used for the graph in Question 6.

11. Describe the shape of this graph. Use the questions in Question 7 to help you tell the story of the data.

12. **A.** Use your graph to estimate the median life span for the 2007 data.
    B. Use your data to find the median life span.

13. Use the graphs to help you compare the two sets of data. What do the graphs tell you about the length of the life spans in the two data sets?

14. What do you think caused the changes in life spans?

Student Guide - page 275 *(Answers on p. 82)*

graphs they have made. Students will graph the Percent of Deaths on the vertical axis. Make sure students scale this axis appropriately. One suggestion is to number by 4s. Graph the Age in Years on the horizontal axis. Number the lines of the graph using the first number of each interval. Spaces between the lines represent the bins or intervals. Students build the bars in these spaces to show that the data falls within the interval (see Figure 7).

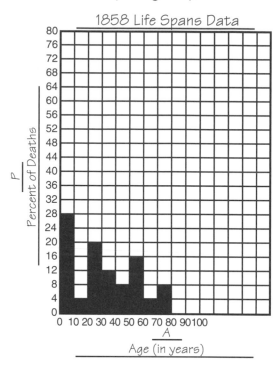

Figure 7: *Graph of life spans from the 1858 data*

The *Graphing Life Spans* Transparency Master shows a sample graph of this data. Before you continue, use students' graphs of the 1858 data to make sure they understand the procedure for graphing. Students can discuss *Question 7* in small groups and then report their conclusions to the whole class. Encourage students to connect the shape of the graph to the data. For example, they can say that the tallest bar at the beginning of the graph tells us that many people in this set died in early childhood.

Question 8 asks students to estimate first the median life span in the 1858 data and then find the median. Since half the data falls within the first three bars, they can estimate that the median age at death is near 30 years old. To find the median, students will need to order the ages from youngest to oldest and find the middle value (27 years).

Students can work independently or in small groups to complete *Questions 9–12.* Figures 8 and 9 show the data table and graph for the 1997 data. Remind

1997 Life Spans Data

A Age (in years)	N Number of Deaths		Fraction of Deaths	Percent of Deaths (to the Nearest Percent)
	Tallies	Number		
0–9		0	$\frac{0}{50}$	0%
10–19	I	1	$\frac{1}{50}$	2%
20–29		0	$\frac{0}{50}$	0%
30–39	I	1	$\frac{1}{50}$	2%
40–49	I	1	$\frac{1}{50}$	2%
50–59	II	2	$\frac{2}{50}$	4%
60–69	卌 II	7	$\frac{7}{50}$	14%
70–79	卌 卌 III	13	$\frac{13}{50}$	26%
80–89	卌 卌 卌 IIII	19	$\frac{19}{50}$	38%
90–99	卌 I	6	$\frac{6}{50}$	12%

Figure 8: *1997 data table*

students to use the same scales they used for the 1858 graph so they can easily compare the graphs. You can also assign *Questions 9–12* for homework.

In *Question 11* students are asked to describe the 1997 graph. They should see that the bars are taller as you move to the right on the graph and that there are no bars or very short bars in the first five intervals. This tells us that most people in the 1997 data set lived longer than 50 years and very few people died under the age of 50.

Students are asked to compare the two graphs in *Question 13.* You can use the *Graphing Life Spans* transparency as you discuss this question. Since the shapes of the two graphs are different, the life spans of people in these two samples are also different. On the 1858 graph, there is a tall bar at the very beginning of the graph. The rest of the graph is made up of shorter bars. The tallest bar represents deaths of young children. There are no bars past the age of 80. The 1997 graph shows no deaths for young children. There are short bars in the intervals for the ages 10–60 years. The tallest bars represent deaths between the ages of 70 and 90 years. A small percentage of this data set lived into their 90s. Comparing these two graphs and, therefore, these two data sets, students can say that many more people in the 1858 data set died as children and very few lived long lives. In general, the people in the 1997 data set lived longer lives. This change can also be seen by comparing medians. The median life span of the people in the 1858 data set was 27 years, and

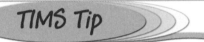

TIMS Tip

The tallies on the 1997 data table should equal 50 and the sum of the percents should equal 100%.

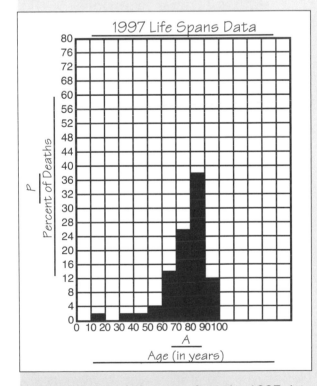

Figure 9: *Graph of life spans from the 1997 data*

the median life span of the people in the 1997 data set was 79.5 years *(Question 12).*

As students answer *Question 14,* they should think about possible reasons for the change in shape of the two graphs. Students should understand that in the 1800s, many children died. Of those who survived childhood, many died early in life because of poor living conditions and disease. In the 1900s, living conditions began to improve in the United States. Changes that have had a significant impact on human life spans include the improvement of sanitation conditions that prevented the spread of infectious diseases. These changes include increased use of window screens, accessibility to pure drinking water, and appropriate treatment of raw sewage. There were also improvements in medical care, such as the development of antibiotics that were used to treat infectious diseases. Thus, fewer children died and people now live longer lives.

Homework and Practice

- Assign DPP Bit G before the activity for a quick review of converting fractions to decimals to percents.
- Students can complete the data table and graph for the 1997 data *(Questions 9–12)* as homework.
- Assign DPP item H as a review of geometry in preparation for the midyear assessment.
- Assign Part 2 of the Home Practice, which provides practice with estimation and computation.

Answers for Part 2 of the Home Practice are in the Answer Key at the end of this lesson and at the end of this unit.

Extension

Collect additional life span data. Choose one or more time frames that your class is interested in studying. You may choose to look for data on people who lived during the 1800s and 1900s and compare your data with the data in the lesson. You can gather data from obituaries in newspapers as described in the *Student Guide* or you can gather data from cemeteries. Using information from the headstones, record the birth and death dates for at least 30 to 40 people in each time frame you choose to study. Time frames should not overlap. Graph this data and compare it to the graphs you have already made.

Name _____ Date _____

Unit 8 Home Practice

PART 1 *Triangle Flash Cards: All the Facts*
Study for the test on the multiplication and division facts. Take home the flash cards for the facts you need to study.

Ask a family member to choose one flash card at a time. To quiz you on a multiplication fact, he or she should cover the corner containing the highest number. Multiply the two uncovered numbers.

To quiz you on a division fact, your family member can cover one of the smaller numbers. One of the smaller numbers is circled. The other has a square around it. Use the two uncovered numbers to solve a division fact.

Ask your family member to mix up the multiplication and division facts. He or she should sometimes cover the highest number, sometimes cover the circled number, and sometimes cover the number in the square.

Your teacher will tell you when the test on the facts will be given.

PART 2 **Practicing the Operations**
1. Use paper and pencil to solve the following problems. Estimate each answer to make sure it is reasonable. Show your work on a separate sheet of paper.
   A. $72 \times 61 =$ B. $0.43 + 7.6 =$ C. $3804 \div 7 =$ D. $61 \times 0.29 =$

2. Estimate the following answers. Describe your strategy for each.
   A. $78,000 \div 40$

   B. $104,000 \div 27$

   C. 9821×14

   D. $178 \times 324,000$

APPLICATIONS: AN ASSESSMENT UNIT   DAB • Grade 5 • Unit 8 **127**

Discovery Assignment Book - page 127 (Answers on p. 82)

At a Glance

Math Facts and Daily Practice and Problems

Assign DPP items G–H, which review fractions, decimals, percents, and geometry.

Part 1. Life Spans

1. Read and discuss the vignette and the data tables on the *Life Spans* Activity Pages in the *Student Guide.* *(Question 1)*
2. Discuss why graphing this data, as presented, would be difficult. Use the prompts in the Lesson Guide to lead a discussion on how to graph the data. *(Question 2)*
3. Introduce binning of data. Explain that this strategy allows work with data that has a broad range. It also makes it easier to see patterns in data. *(Question 3)*
4. Discuss use of percents to compare data when each data set has a different number of data points. *(Question 4)*

Part 2. Graphing Life Spans Data

1. Fill in data tables for the 1858 data using the *Life Spans Data Tables* Activity Page in the *Discovery Assignment Book.* Convert fractions to percents. *(Question 5)*
2. Make a bar graph of this data. Use the transparency to make sure students understand how to scale both axes. Make sure students build the bars between the lines to indicate the bins. *(Question 6)*
3. Discuss the shape of the graph. Use the *Student Guide* prompts to connect the shape of the graph to the data. *(Question 7)*
4. Students find the average life span in the 1858 data. *(Question 8)*
5. Students complete *Questions 9–12* that ask them to organize, graph, and analyze the 1997 data.
6. Discuss *Questions 13–14.* Compare the two sets of data using the graphs and medians.

Homework

1. For homework, students can complete the data table and graph for 1997 data. They find the median age at death for this data. *(Questions 9–12)*
2. Assign Part 2 of the Home Practice.

Extension

Collect additional life span data. Choose one or more different time frames. Gather data for 30 to 40 people from obituaries or cemeteries. Graph this data and compare it to the graphs already made.

Answer Key is on pages 81–82.

Notes:

Graphing Life Spans

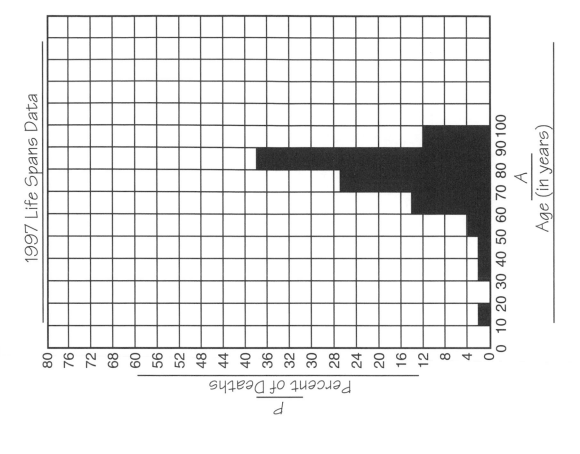

1997 Life Spans Data

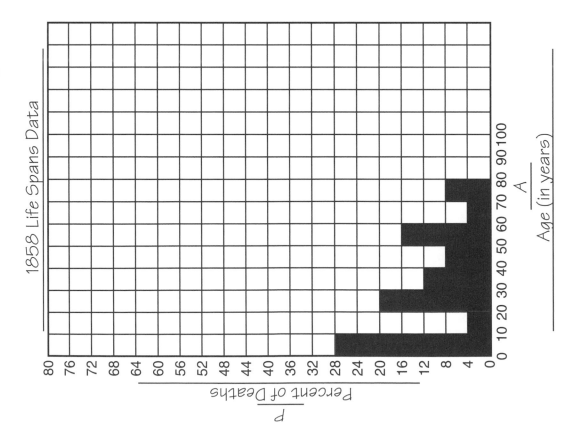

1858 Life Spans Data

Transparency Master

Copyright © Kendall/Hunt Publishing Company

Student Guide (p. 273)

Life Spans

1. Answers will vary. See discussion in Lesson Guide 5.*

Life Spans

The students in Mr. Moreno's classroom are studying the history of the United States. They learned that the United States changed rapidly during the 1900s. During this time, many people began working in factories instead of on farms. Living conditions and sanitation improved for most people. At the same time, the discovery of antibiotics and other improvements in medical care changed the way doctors treated diseases.

The students wondered if these changes had any effect on the length of time people lived. Mr. Moreno suggested that they collect information on the life spans of people before these changes occurred. They could then compare them with the life spans of people after these changes occurred. The students decided to compare the life spans of a set of people who lived during the 1800s to the life spans of a set of people who lived during the 1900s.

Brandon and David went to the library to collect data. Brandon looked for obituaries in old newspapers. He looked through newspapers from the year 1858 and found 25 death notices that listed the names of the people who died and their age at death. He wrote down the age of each person: 56 yr, 1 yr 3 mo, 54 yr, 9 mo, 27 yr, 42 yr, 2½ mo, 5 yr, 38 yr, 34 yr, 79 yr, 59 yr, 76 yr, infant, 21 yr, 25 yr, 24 yr, 19 yr, 30 yr, 62 yr, 51 yr, 43 yr, 20 yr, 1 yr, and 5 yr.

David looked in more recent newspapers. He found 50 obituaries that gave the age at death. He wrote down these ages, which were all given in years: 75, 88, 84, 79, 85, 86, 51, 77, 85, 88, 88, 71, 84, 85, 89, 92, 77, 97, 80, 60, 95, 62, 85, 64, 44, 74, 62, 87, 81, 73, 89, 15, 96, 84, 72, 89, 84, 90, 88, 50, 68, 72, 75, 63, 90, 65, 38, 77, 79, and 73. All the people in David's data set died in February of 2007.

Discuss

David and Brandon shared their data with the class.

1. Compare the two sets of life spans. What do you notice about the length of the life spans in the 1858 data and in the 2007 data?

Life Spans   SG • Grade 5 • Unit 8 • Lesson 5 **273**

Student Guide - page 273

Student Guide (p. 274)

2. Answers will vary. See discussion in Lesson Guide 5.*

3. Suggested intervals are 0–9 yr, 10–19 yr, 20–29 yr, 30–39 yr, 40–49 yr, 50–59 yr, 60–69 yr, 70–79 yr.*

4.* **A.** 25 life spans

   B. 50 life spans

   C. Use percents to compare the data.

5. See the data table in Figure 6 in Lesson Guide 5.*

6. See the graph in Figure 7 in Lesson Guide 5.*

2. The students in Mr. Moreno's class found it difficult to compare the two sets of data as David and Brandon reported it. They decided to make two graphs to display the data. How can you set up the graphs to tell the story of the data?

Mr. Moreno suggested that the students **bin** their data. He explained that when you bin data, you look at how data falls within equal intervals. For example, if you measure the height of each person in the class, you can group the data into bins: For example, heights of 120–129 centimeters, 130–139 centimeters, 140–149 centimeters, 150–159 centimeters, and 160–169 centimeters. The number of heights in each bin is recorded.

3. **A.** What intervals can you use to bin the life span data? (Hint: Listing the ages on a separate sheet of paper may help you choose your bins.)

   B. What are some reasons to bin data?

4. The students binned the data and recorded the number of life spans in each interval. They knew they had a different number of people in each data set.

   A. How many life spans are in the 1858 data?

   B. How many life spans are in the 1997 data?

   C. What strategies can the students use to compare the data in the two sets?

5. Use the 1858 data to complete a data table like the one shown below. You may use the Life Spans Data Tables Activity Page in the Discovery Assignment Book. (Hint: To tally the data, list the ages on a separate sheet of paper. Then you can check off each number as you tally.)

A Age (in years)	N Number of Deaths		Fraction of Deaths	Percent of Deaths (to the Nearest Percent)
	Tallies	Number		

Graph

6. For this type of data, mathematicians usually use a bar graph.
   • Make a bar graph of this data.

274 SG • Grade 5 • Unit 8 • Lesson 5   Life Spans

Student Guide - page 274

*Answers and/or discussion are included in the Lesson Guide.

Student Guide - page 275

- Plot the Percent of Deaths on the vertical axis.
- Plot the Age in Years on the horizontal axis.
- Draw the bars between the lines to show that most of the ages fall between the numbers on the horizontal axis.
- When you start graphing the data, your graph might look like the graph to the right.

7. Describe the shape of your graph. The shape of the graph tells the story of the data. Use these questions to help you.
- Are all the bars about the same height, or are some bars much taller than others?
- Where are the tallest bars—at the beginning, middle, or end of the graph?
- What do the heights of the bars tell you about life spans in this set of data?

8. A. Use your graph to estimate the median life span for the 1858 data.
   B. Use your data to find the median life span.

9. Use the 2007 data to complete a data table like the one in Question 5.

10. Make a bar graph of the 2007 data.
- Plot the Age in Years on the horizontal axis and the Percent of Deaths on the vertical axis.
- Use the same scales you used for the graph in Question 6.

11. Describe the shape of this graph. Use the questions in Question 7 to help you tell the story of the data.

12. A. Use your graph to estimate the median life span for the 2007 data.
    B. Use your data to find the median life span.

13. Use the graphs to help you compare the two sets of data. What do the graphs tell you about the length of the life spans in the two data sets?

14. What do you think caused the changes in life spans?

Life Spans — SG • Grade 5 • Unit 8 • Lesson 5 **275**

Student Guide - page 275

Discovery Assignment Book - page 127

Name _____ Date _____

Unit 8 Home Practice

PART 1 Triangle Flash Cards: All the Facts
Study for the test on the multiplication and division facts. Take home the flash cards for the facts you need to study.

Ask a family member to choose one flash card at a time. To quiz you on a multiplication fact, he or she should cover the corner containing the highest number. Multiply the two uncovered numbers.

To quiz you on a division fact, your family member can cover one of the smaller numbers. One of the smaller numbers is circled. The other has a square around it. Use the two uncovered numbers to solve a division fact.

Ask your family member to mix up the multiplication and division facts. He or she should sometimes cover the highest number, sometimes cover the circled number, and sometimes cover the number in the square.

Your teacher will tell you when the test on the facts will be given.

PART 2 Practicing the Operations
1. Use paper and pencil to solve the following problems. Estimate each answer to make sure it is reasonable. Show your work on a separate sheet of paper.
   A. 72 × 61 = B. 0.43 + 7.6 = C. 3804 ÷ 7 = D. 61 × 0.29 =

2. Estimate the following answers. Describe your strategy for each.
   A. 78,000 ÷ 40
   B. 104,000 ÷ 27
   C. 9821 × 14
   D. 178 × 324,000

APPLICATIONS: AN ASSESSMENT UNIT   DAB • Grade 5 • Unit 8 **127**

Student Guide (p. 275)

7. Answers will vary. The tallest bar is at the beginning of the graph which tells us that many people in this data set died in childhood. All the other bars are shorter and there are no bars after 80 years of age indicating that few people lived long lives.*

8.*A. About 30 years old.
   B. 27 years old.

9. See the data table in Figure 8 in Lesson Guide 5.*

10. See the graph in Figure 9 in Lesson Guide 5.*

11. Answers will vary. There isn't a bar in the first interval indicating there weren't any deaths during early childhood in this data set. There are no bars or very short bars between the ages of 10 and 50, so very few people died under the age of 50. The bars between the ages of 50 and 90 years get larger as you move to the right on the graph. The tallest bars are between the ages of 70 and 90. These bars tell us that most people in the 1997 data set lived long lives.*

12. A. Answers will vary slightly. About 80 years.
    B. 79.5 years

13. Answers will vary. See the discussion in Lesson Guide 5.*

14. Answers will vary. See the discussion in Lesson Guide 5.*

Discovery Assignment Book (p. 127)

Home Practice[†]

Part 2. Practicing the Operations

1. A. 4392   B. 8.03
   C. 543 R3   D. 17.69

2. Answers will vary. Possible strategies are shown.
   A. $80,000 \div 40 = 2000$
   B. $100,000 \div 25 = 4000$
   C. $10,000 \times 14 = 140,000$
   D. $200 \times 300,000 = 60,000,000$

*Answers and/or discussion are included in the Lesson Guide.
[†]Answers for all the Home Practice in the *Discovery Assignment Book* are at the end of the unit.

Lesson 6

Comparing Lives of Animals and Soap Bubbles

Estimated Class Sessions

3

Lesson Overview

This lab extends students' Lesson 5 investigations of the life spans of people. Students collect, graph, and analyze data on the length of time soap bubbles live. They compare the graphs from their classroom experiment showing the "age at death" of bubbles to graphs showing the age at death of animals. They are assessed on their abilities to collect, graph, and analyze data and to use percents in the context of an experiment.

Key Content

- Collecting, organizing, graphing, and analyzing data.
- Using numerical variables.
- Making and interpreting bar graphs using binned data.
- Translating between graphs and real-world events.
- Using fractions, decimals, and percents to represent the same quantity.
- Connecting mathematics and science to real-world situations.
- Using the Student Rubric: *Telling* to self-assess communication skills.

Math Facts

DPP items I, K, and M review math facts.

Homework

1. Assign some or all of the review problems in Lesson 7 for homework.
2. Assign Parts 3 and 4 of the Home Practice.

Assessment

1. Grade the lab by assigning points to drawing the picture, collecting and recording the data, graphing, and solving problems.
2. Score student responses to *Questions 10–12* using the Telling dimension of the *TIMS Multidimensional Rubric*.

Materials List

Supplies and Copies

Student	Teacher
Supplies for Each Student • calculator **Supplies for Each Student Group** • small jar of bubble solution • bubble wand • stopwatch or watch that measures seconds • paper towels	**Supplies**
Copies • 1 copy of *Centimeter Graph Paper* per student (*Unit Resource Guide* Page 67)	**Copies/Transparencies** • 1 transparency of *Soap Bubbles Data Table,* optional (*Discovery Assignment Book* Page 143) • 1 transparency of *Centimeter Graph Paper,* optional (*Unit Resource Guide* Page 67) • 1 copy of *TIMS Multidimensional Rubric* (*Teacher Implementation Guide,* Assessment section)

All blackline masters including assessment, transparency, and DPP masters are also on the Teacher Resource CD.

Student Books

Comparing Lives of Animals and Soap Bubbles (*Student Guide* Pages 276–279)
Student Rubric: *Telling* (*Student Guide* Appendix C and Inside Back Cover)
Soap Bubbles Data Table (*Discovery Assignment Book* Page 143), optional

Daily Practice and Problems and Home Practice

DPP items I–N (*Unit Resource Guide* Pages 19–22)
Home Practice Parts 3–4 (*Discovery Assignment Book* Page 128)

Note: Classrooms whose pacing differs significantly from the suggested pacing of the units should use the Math Facts Calendar in Section 4 of the *Facts Resource Guide* to ensure students receive the complete math facts program.

Assessment Tools

TIMS Multidimensional Rubric (*Teacher Implementation Guide,* Assessment section)

Suggestions for using the DPPs are on page 90.

I. Bit: Fact Practice II (URG p. 19)

Find *n* to make each number sentence true.

A. $10 \times n = 90$ B. $16 \div 2 = n$

C. $3 \times 5 = n$ D. $28 \div 4 = n$

E. $4 \times n = 36$ F. $50 \div n = 10$

G. $6 \times 2 = n$ H. $24 \div 3 = n$

I. $7 \times n = 63$

J. Challenge: Letter Chances
(URG p. 20)

1. Write down your full name (first, last, and, if you like, middle name). If you cut out all the letters in your names and put them in a bowl, list the probability of choosing each letter that appears in your name. For example, if your name is Roberto Ruiz, the chance of choosing an R is $\frac{3}{11}$. The chance of choosing an O is $\frac{2}{11}$. The chance of choosing a B is $\frac{1}{11}$.

2. What is the probability you will choose a vowel from the letters in your name?

3. What is the probability you will choose a letter in the first half of the alphabet (A–M)?

4. What is the probability you will choose one of the last five letters in the alphabet?

K. Bit: Fact Practice III (URG p. 20)

Find *n* to make each number sentence true.

A. $70 \times 6 = n$ B. $90 \times 90 = n$

C. $3000 \div 6 = n$ D. $14,000 \div 200 = n$

E. $40 \times 400 = n$ F. $56,000 \div 80 = n$

G. $30 \times n = 180$ H. $5000 \times 9 = n$

I. $800 \div 10 = n$

L. Task: Adding and Subtracting Fractions (URG p. 21)

A. $\frac{3}{6} + \frac{2}{6} =$ B. $\frac{2}{3} + \frac{1}{5} =$

C. $\frac{1}{4} - \frac{1}{6} =$ D. $\frac{5}{8} - \frac{1}{4} =$

E. $\frac{3}{8} - \frac{1}{8} =$ F. $\frac{1}{2} - \frac{2}{5} =$

M. Bit: Fact Practice IV (URG p. 21)

Find *n* to make each number sentence true. Then name one other fact in the same fact family.

A. $9 \times 2 = n$ B. $30 \div 5 = n$

C. $7 \times 7 = n$ D. $32 \div 8 = n$

E. $10 \times 7 = n$ F. $6 \times 8 = n$

G. $27 \div 3 = n$ H. $8 \times 9 = n$

I. $24 \div 4 = n$

N. Challenge: A Busy School Day!
(URG p. 22)

1. On an average school day, Jackie spends six hours in school. What percent of her day is spent in school?

2. Jackie practices piano one hour on a school day. What fraction of the day does she spend practicing piano?

3. Jackie spends $\frac{1}{3}$ of a day sleeping. How many hours does she sleep?

4. What fraction of Jackie's day is left after school, piano, and sleep? More or less than $\frac{1}{2}$ of a day?

5. Write a similar story using your own daily activities.

Comparing Lives of Animals and Soap Bubbles

Lives of Animals

The shape of a graph can give important information. In Lesson 5 you graphed data on the life spans of people in the United States. You compared the shapes of two graphs. Biologists also gather similar information about animals. They collect data on the age at death of many animals of the same species. Once graphed, these data give important information to the scientist about that species.

The following are brief descriptions of the lives of three different kinds of animals:

Humans. Humans nurture their young until they are old enough to care for themselves. However, babies are at greater risk of illness and disease because their immune systems are still developing. Humans die from disease and accidents as they age, but modern medicine has controlled many diseases, so the majority of people live a long time.

American robins. Robins care for their young until they are old enough to fly and gather food for themselves. From the time they leave the nest, robins of all ages are equally likely to be eaten by predators or to die from accidents. Chance has a much greater effect on how long robins live than it does for other kinds of organisms.

Oysters. Early in life, oysters are very small and have thin shells. Most are eaten by predators when they are very young. As adults with thick shells, surviving oysters live for a very long time.

Student Guide - page 276

---

1. The following three graphs show the age at which these animals are most likely to die. Find the graph that matches the description for each animal: humans, American robins, and oysters.

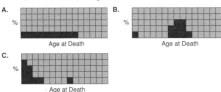

Experimenting with Soap Bubbles

Often, scientific experiments are limited by the conditions in a laboratory. As scientists in a classroom, you cannot collect data on the life spans of many kinds of animals. Biologists have found that the shape of a graph showing the "age at death" of soap bubbles resembles the shape of similar graphs for some animals.

In this experiment, you will collect data on the life spans or "age at death" of soap bubbles. Using these data, you will make graphs similar to those you made of the life spans of people in Lesson 5. Then the graphs from your soap bubble data will be compared to the three graphs shown in Question 1.

To collect the data for this experiment, measure the time that each bubble lives. Then find the percentage of the bubbles that live for a given time.

2. Try out your bubble solution. Observe the bubbles. Catch some with your wand, and observe them until they pop. What variables are involved in the experiment? What variables do you think affect the life span of a soap bubble?

Student Guide - page 277 (Answers on p. 94)

Part 1   Launching the Investigation

Read and discuss the descriptions of the lives of different kinds of animals in the first section of the *Comparing Lives of Animals and Soap Bubbles* Activity Pages in the *Student Guide*. ***Question 1*** asks students to match three descriptions of the life spans of three kinds of animals with three different graphs showing the percent of animals that die at any given age. Each graph has a characteristic shape. Be sure students can correctly identify each graph.

Graph A matches the description of the life spans of American robins, since robins of all ages are equally likely to die. Graph B displays the life spans of humans since tall bars to the right indicate that the majority of humans live a long time. Graph C represents the life spans of oysters, since the bars to the left tell us that most oysters die at a young age. The shape of these graphs will be compared to the shape of a graph showing the percent of bubbles that burst after any given number of seconds.

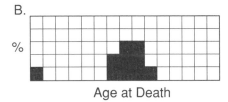

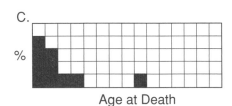

Figure 10: *Graph A is for American robins, Graph B for humans, and Graph C for oysters.*

The second section in the *Student Guide*, Experimenting with Soap Bubbles, discusses the experiment's procedure. ***Question 2*** directs students to observe a few bubbles and consider the experiment's variables. The two main variables, the time at which a bubble pops and the percent of bubbles that pop after any given number of seconds, are analogous to an animal's age at death and the percent of deaths at any given age. The experiment also involves the following variables since they may affect the bubble's life span:

- the type of bubble solution,
- whether the bubble is held on a wand or allowed to drop to the ground,
- the ventilation in the room,
- the air temperature,
- the humidity, and
- the size of a bubble.

In **Question 3,** students develop a plan for collecting data.

- To measure accurately a bubble's life span, they must first decide when its life begins and ends. To find out how long a bubble will live if it does not hit the ground or another object, they should catch the bubbles on the wand. The moment the bubble lands on the wand and the moment the bubble pops can be defined as the beginning and end of a bubble's life *(Question 3A).*

- *Question 3B* asks for fixed variables. The type of bubble solution should be the same for all bubbles and each bubble should be held the same way on the wand (either up or down). Because the temperature, humidity, and movement of the air affect the time bubbles last, it is best to time the bubbles in the classroom away from open windows, air conditioners, or heating vents.

- Since often one blow makes many bubbles, students will only be able to select one bubble from any group to time with the stopwatch. They should try to select bubbles of the same size and should not choose "double" bubbles *(Question 3C).*

- *Question 3D* asks students to select a sample size. Twenty or 25 bubbles provide enough data to analyze and both are good numbers to use when finding percents.

- Three students per group work well for this lab. One student can blow the bubbles and catch them on the wand, one can time the bubbles, and one can record the data *(Question 3E).*

Part 2 **Drawing the Picture and Collecting the Data**

Question 4 directs students to draw a picture that shows the procedures and identifies the variables. Use the pictures to check that students have a clear idea of the procedures and the variables involved in the experiment. See Figure 11 for an example of a student's labeled drawing. Then each group should proceed with the investigation as independently as

3. Develop a plan for collecting reliable data on the life spans of soap bubbles. Consider the following:
   A. When does a bubble's "life" begin and end? (When will you start and stop the timer?)
   B. What variables should be held fixed?
   C. Sometimes, many bubbles are made at once. Which bubbles will be part of your sample?
   D. How many bubbles will you time? (How many bubbles will be in your sample?)
   E. What will each member of your group do to help collect the data?

4. Draw a picture of the experiment. Label the important variables. Show your procedure.

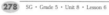

5. Time a few bubbles. Will you need to bin your data?

6. You will make a bar graph of the life spans of soap bubbles. Use what you have learned from Question 5 to predict what the shape of your bar graph will look like. Make a sketch, or write a description for your prediction. Use these questions to help you:
   • Will all the bars be about the same height, or will some bars be much taller than others?
   • Where will the tallest bars be—at the beginning, middle, or end of the graph?
   • Will your graph look like one of those shown for humans, robins, or oysters?

7. Draw a data table like the one that follows, or use a copy of the *Soap Bubbles Data Table* Activity Page from the *Discovery Assignment Book.* Choose time intervals such as 5 or 10 seconds to bin the data. Fill in the first column of the data table with the intervals. Be sure the intervals do not overlap and are the same size.

278 SG • Grade 5 • Unit 8 • Lesson 6   Comparing Lives of Animals and Soap Bubbles

Student Guide - page 278 (Answers on p. 94)

Soap Bubbles Data Table

Life Spans of Soap Bubbles

t Time in Seconds	Tallies	N Number of Bubbles	P Percent of Bubbles

Comparing Lives of Animals and Soap Bubbles   DAB • Grade 5 • Unit 8 • Lesson 6 **143**

Discovery Assignment Book - page 143 (Answers on p. 96)

Life Spans of Soap Bubbles

t Time in Seconds	Tallies	N Number of Bubbles	P Percent of Bubbles
0.00 – 9.99		0	0%
10.00 –19.99		0	0%
20.00 – 29.99		0	0%
30.00 – 39.99	ⅢⅠ	5	25%
40.00 – 49.99	ⅢⅠ II	7	35%
50.00 – 59.99	ⅢⅠ II	7	35%
60.00 – 69.99	I	1	5%
70.00 – 79.99		0	0%

Figure 12: *Sample data for 20 bubbles*

possible so you can assess their abilities to carry out an experiment.

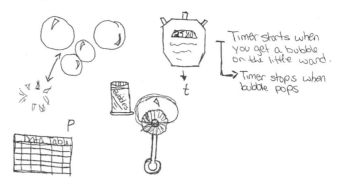

Figure 11: *Sample of a labeled student picture*

Before students begin collecting data, they should time a few bubbles *(Question 5)*. Since the number of seconds the bubbles live can vary greatly, students will need to bin the data. *Question 6* asks them to use this preliminary data to predict the shape of a graph of the bubbles' life spans by drawing a sketch or describing the graph in words. The question prompts students to connect the length of time the bubbles last to bars on a graph. They can use the graphs in the *Student Guide* that show the life spans of American robins, oysters, and humans as examples.

The preliminary data from *Question 5* will also give students an idea of possible values for the length of time bubbles will last using your brand of bubble solution and given the conditions in your room. Before students collect and record data, they should fill in the first column of their data tables with intervals *(Question 7)*. Students will need to bin the data so the scale of the graph is reasonable and so they can look for patterns. We recommend that students use intervals of five or ten seconds. The sample data in Figure 12 is for 20 bubbles using a commercially available bubble solution. The data table's first column shows intervals of 10 seconds that are all the same size and do not overlap.

TIMS Tip

Avoid overlapping intervals. For example, if intervals such as 1–10 seconds and 10–20 seconds are used, it is not clear where to make a tally mark for 10 seconds. Another common mistake is to make the last interval "greater than 80 seconds," which is not the same size as the other intervals. Note also that intervals in the sample data table are given to the nearest hundredth of a second to correspond with the readings on a stopwatch. If you only measure the time to the nearest second or tenth of a second, write the intervals accordingly.

Part 3 Graphing the Data

Question 9 directs students to make a graph of the data with time (in seconds) on the horizontal axis and the percent of bubbles on the vertical axis. Since this is an assessment lab, students should complete their graphs as independently as possible. Figure 13 is a graph of the sample data. Note the horizontal axis is scaled by 10s since the width of each interval (bin) in the data table is 10 seconds.

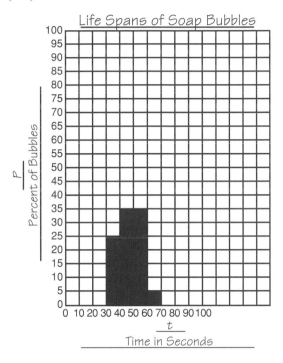

Figure 13: *Graph of the sample data*

Part 4 Analyzing the Data

Questions 10–11 ask students to analyze the shapes of their graphs. To help students plan their responses, review the Student Rubric: *Telling*. Tell them you will use the rubric when you score their work. All bars on the graph in Figure 13 lie between 30 and 70 seconds and three of the four bars are similar in height. This tells us that the bubbles lived for a long time and all burst after about the same amount of time. Although no bubbles died at a young age, this graph is similar to the graph for humans in the *Student Guide* since, like bubbles, humans are likely to live for a relatively long time and many die at about the same age *(Question 12)*. Note that although we found that the shape of the graphs for the bubbles' life spans usually resembles the graph for humans, different conditions and bubble solutions may result in graphs with different shapes.

Life Spans of Soap Bubbles

t Time in Seconds	Tallies	N Number of Bubbles	P Percent of Bubbles

8. Collect your data. Fill in your data table.

G r a p h

9. Make a bar graph of your data. Graph time on the horizontal axis and the percent of bubbles on the vertical axis. Number the lines on the horizontal axis with the first value of each interval.

Explore

10. Describe the shape of your graph. What does it tell you about the life spans of bubbles? Consider the following:
   • Did most of the bubbles burst immediately with only a few lasting for a long time?
   • Were the bubbles as likely to last 10 seconds as 15, 25, or 50 seconds?
   • Did most of the bubbles live for a long time and burst after about the same amount of time?

11. Compare the shape of your graph to the shape you predicted in Question 6. Was your prediction correct? Why or why not?

12. Compare your graph to the graphs of the life spans of humans, American robins, and oysters in the *Student Guide*. Which of these three graphs is most like your graph? Explain.

Comparing Lives of Animals and Soap Bubbles   SG • Grade 5 • Unit 8 • Lesson 6   **279**

Student Guide - page 279 (Answers on p. 95)

Journal Prompt

What mathematical skills does a biologist need to study the life spans of animals?

Discovery Assignment Book - page 128 *(Answers on p. 95)*

Math Facts

DPP items I, K, and M provide practice with the multiplication and division facts using variables in number sentences.

Homework and Practice

- Assign some or all of the review problems in Lesson 7 for homework.

- DPP items J, L, and N review probability and operations with fractions, decimals, and percents. Assign these items as practice in preparation for the Midyear Test in Lesson 8.

- Assign Parts 3 and 4 of the Home Practice, which review the concepts for the midyear test.

Answers for Parts 3 and 4 of the Home Practice are in the Answer Key at the end of this lesson and at the end of this unit.

Assessment

To grade the lab, assign a given number of points to each part and base your grade for each part on the following criteria:

1. Drawing the picture
   - Is the procedure clearly illustrated?
   - Are the variables labeled?

2. Collecting and recording the data
   - Are the intervals in the first column correct? (They all should be the same size and should not overlap.)
   - Are the correct units of measure (seconds) included?
   - Does the sum of the number of bubbles in the third column equal the number of bubbles in the sample?
   - Are the percents correct?

3. Graphing the data
   - Does the graph have a title?
   - Are the axes scaled correctly and labeled clearly?
   - Does the scale on the horizontal axis match the intervals in the first column of the data table?
   - Are the bars drawn correctly?

4. Solving the problems
   - Are the answers correct based on the data?
   - Are the answers, including the explanations, clear and complete?

Score student responses to **Questions 10–12** using the Telling dimension of the *TIMS Multidimensional Rubric.* To help you use the rubric to score students' work, consider the following questions:

- Did students clearly describe the shapes of their graphs?

- Did students connect the shapes of the graphs to the data? Did they explain how the heights of the bars reflect the life spans of the bubbles?

- Did students compare their graphs to their predictions in **Question 6?** Did they tell why their predictions were correct or incorrect?

- Did they compare their graphs to the graphs of the American robin, oysters, and humans? Did each student explain why the shape of his or her graph is like the shape of one of these three graphs? Are the shapes of the graphs connected to the life spans of the animals and soap bubbles?

Extension

- In a class discussion, compare each group's graphs with one another. Are most graphs similar? Why or why not? If all groups used the same bubble solution and followed the same procedures, all graphs should look similar to one another.

- After you compare the groups' graphs with one another, combine the data from all groups and make a graph that shows the percent of bubbles that live for any given length of time. Compare the class graph with the groups' graphs. How are they alike? How are they different? Since the class graph and the groups' graphs show the percent of bubbles, the class graph should look similar to the groups' graphs.

- Compare the graphs from this lab with the graphs from Lesson 5 *Life Spans.* How do the two graphs for Lesson 5 compare with the bubbles' graph?

Students can make graphs similar to those they made in class using *Graph Master* or a similar graphing and data analysis program. They enter the number of seconds each bubble "lived" in one column of the data table. Students then use the tally function before asking for a graph. If students choose histogram as the type of graph, the program will ask for the size of the intervals for the horizontal axis. Choosing the interval size will bin the data. Note that the graphs will have the same shape as those the students made in class. However, the variable on the vertical axis will be frequency, or number of bubbles, instead of percent of bubbles.

Math Facts and Daily Practice and Problems

Complete DPP items I–N. Items I, K, and M review math facts. Items J, L, and N review concepts on the midyear test in Lesson 8.

Part 1. Launching the Investigation

1. Discuss the descriptions of the lives of different kinds of animals in the *Comparing Lives of Animals and Soap Bubbles* Lab Pages in the *Student Guide*. Match the descriptions with the graphs in *Question 1*.
2. Students observe a few bubbles. Use *Questions 2–3* to identify the variables and develop the procedure for the lab.

Part 2. Drawing the Picture and Collecting the Data

1. Students draw a picture of the procedures and label the variables. *(Question 4)*
2. Before collecting data, students time a few bubbles and use this information to choose intervals to bin the data and predict the shape of the graph. *(Questions 5–6)*
3. Students fill in the first column of the data table with appropriate intervals. *(Question 7)*
4. Students collect the data and complete the data table. *(Question 8)*

Part 3. Graphing the Data

Students make a bar graph of the data. They will need graph paper. *(Question 9)*

Part 4. Analyzing the Data

Review the Student Rubric: *Telling*. Have students use the rubric to guide them in writing their responses to *Questions 10–12*.

Homework

1. Assign some or all of the review problems in Lesson 7 for homework.
2. Assign Parts 3 and 4 of the Home Practice.

Assessment

1. Grade the lab by assigning points to drawing the picture, collecting and recording the data, graphing, and solving problems.
2. Score student responses to *Questions 10–12* using the Telling dimension of the *TIMS Multidimensional Rubric*.

Extension

1. Compare the graphs from each group. Discuss similarities and differences.
2. Combine the data from all the groups' graphs. Discuss similarities and differences.
3. Compare the graphs from this lab with the graphs in Lesson 5.

Connection

Have students use *Graph Master* or another graphing program to make their graphs.

Answer Key is on pages 94–96.

Notes:

Student Guide (p. 277)

1.* **A.** robins

B. humans

C. oysters

2. Time at which the bubbles pop and percent of bubbles that pop after any given number of seconds. Other variables that affect the life span of a bubble: Type of bubble solution, whether the bubble is held on a wand or allowed to drop to the ground, ventilation in the room, air temperature, humidity, and size of bubble.*

---

1. The following three graphs show the age at which these animals are most likely to die. Find the graph that matches the description for each animal: humans, American robins, and oysters.

A.

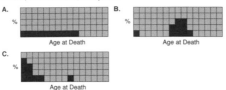

B.

C.

Experimenting with Soap Bubbles

Often, scientific experiments are limited by the conditions in a laboratory. As scientists in a classroom, you cannot collect data on the life spans of many kinds of animals. Biologists have found that the shape of a graph showing the "age at death" of soap bubbles resembles the shape of similar graphs for some animals.

In this experiment, you will collect data on the life spans or "age at death" of soap bubbles. Using these data, you will make graphs similar to those you made of the life spans of people in Lesson 5. Then the graphs from your soap bubble data will be compared to the three graphs shown in Question 1.

To collect the data for this experiment, measure the time that each bubble lives. Then find the percentage of the bubbles that live for a given time.

Discuss

2. Try out your bubble solution. Observe the bubbles. Catch some with your wand, and observe them until they pop. What variables are involved in the experiment? What variables do you think affect the life span of a soap bubble?

Comparing Lives of Animals and Soap Bubbles   SG • Grade 5 • Unit 8 • Lesson 6   **277**

Student Guide - page 277

Student Guide (p. 278)

3. See Lesson Guide 6 for a description of possible procedures.*

4. See Figure 11 in Lesson Guide 6 for a sample picture.*

5. Yes, intervals will vary.*

6. Descriptions and sketches will vary.

7. See Figure 12 in Lesson Guide 6 for a sample data table.*

---

3. Develop a plan for collecting reliable data on the life spans of soap bubbles. Consider the following:

A. When does a bubble's "life" begin and end? (When will you start and stop the timer?)

B. What variables should be held fixed?

C. Sometimes, many bubbles are made at once. Which bubbles will be part of your sample?

D. How many bubbles will you time? (How many bubbles will be in your sample?)

E. What will each member of your group do to help collect the data?

Draw

4. Draw a picture of the experiment. Label the important variables. Show your procedure.

Collect

5. Time a few bubbles. Will you need to bin your data?

6. You will make a bar graph of the life spans of soap bubbles. Use what you have learned from Question 5 to predict what the shape of your bar graph will look like. Make a sketch, or write a description for your prediction. Use these questions to help you:

• Will all the bars be about the same height, or will some bars be much taller than others?

• Where will the tallest bars be—at the beginning, middle, or end of the graph?

• Will your graph look like one of those shown for humans, robins, or oysters?

7. Draw a data table like the one that follows, or use a copy of the *Soap Bubbles Data Table* Activity Page from the *Discovery Assignment Book*. Choose time intervals such as 5 or 10 seconds to bin the data. Fill in the first column of the data table with the intervals. Be sure the intervals do not overlap and are the same size.

278   SG • Grade 5 • Unit 8 • Lesson 6   Comparing Lives of Animals and Soap Bubbles

Student Guide - page 278

*Answers and/or discussion are included in the Lesson Guide.

Student Guide (p. 279)

8. See Figure 12 in Lesson Guide 6 for a sample data table.*

9. See Figure 13 in Lesson Guide 6 for a sample graph.*

10. For the sample graph in Figure 13, all the bars lie between 30 and 70 seconds and three of the four bars are similar in height. The bubbles all lived for a long time and all burst after about the same amount of time.*

11. Answers will vary.

12. Answers will vary. This graph is similar to the graph for humans in Figure 13 in Lesson Guide 6.*

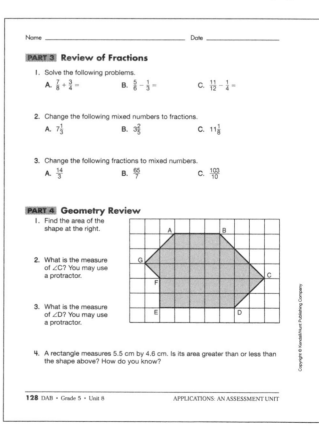

Student Guide - page 279

Discovery Assignment Book (p. 128)

Home Practice†

Part 3. Review of Fractions

1. A. $\frac{13}{8}$ or $1\frac{5}{8}$
   B. $\frac{3}{6}$ or $\frac{1}{2}$
   C. $\frac{8}{12}$ or $\frac{2}{3}$

2. A. $\frac{22}{3}$
   B. $\frac{17}{5}$
   C. $\frac{89}{8}$

3. A. $4\frac{2}{3}$
   B. $9\frac{2}{7}$
   C. $10\frac{3}{10}$

Part 4. Geometry Review

1. 29 sq cm
2. 90°
3. 135°
4. The area of the rectangle is 25.3 sq cm which means it has less area than the shape in Question 1. (5.5 cm × 4.6 cm = 25.3 sq cm)

Discovery Assignment Book - page 128

*Answers and/or discussion are included in the Lesson Guide.
†Answers for all the Home Practice in the *Discovery Assignment Book* are at the end of the unit.

Name _____ Date _____

Soap Bubbles Data Table

Life Spans of Soap Bubbles

t Time in Seconds	Tallies	N Number of Bubbles	P Percent of Bubbles

Comparing Lives of Animals and Soap Bubbles   DAB • Grade 5 • Unit 8 • Lesson 6 **143**

Discovery Assignment Book - page 143

Discovery Assignment Book (p. 143)

Soap Bubbles Data Table

See Figure 12 in Lesson Guide 6 for a sample data table.

Optional Lesson 7

Review Problems

Estimated Class Sessions

1

Lesson Overview

Students solve a variety of multistep word problems that review concepts and skills from the first seven units. They make choices about the tools they use to solve the problems.

Key Content

- Solving multistep word problems.
- Communicating solutions orally and in writing.
- Choosing appropriate methods and tools to calculate (calculator, ruler, or small centiwheels).
- Choosing to find an estimate or an exact answer.
- Representing decimals using circle graphs (centiwheels).
- Drawing and interpreting best-fit lines.
- Using graphs and fractions to express ratios.
- Finding equal ratios.

Key Vocabulary

- compost

Homework

1. Assign some or all of the problems for review, homework, or use for assessment.
2. Assign Part 6 of the Home Practice.

Materials List

Supplies and Copies

Student	Teacher
Supplies for Each Student • centiwheel • ruler • calculator	**Supplies**
Copies • 1 copy of *Centimeter Graph Paper* per student (*Unit Resource Guide* Page 67)	**Copies/Transparencies**

All blackline masters including assessment, transparency, and DPP masters are also on the Teacher Resource CD.

Student Books
Review Problems (*Student Guide* Pages 280–281)

Daily Practice and Problems and Home Practice
Home Practice Part 6 (*Discovery Assignment Book* Page 130)

Note: Classrooms whose pacing differs significantly from the suggested pacing of the units should use the Math Facts Calendar in Section 4 of the *Facts Resource Guide* to ensure students receive the complete math facts program.

This problem set can serve several purposes. It gives students opportunities to practice choosing appropriate methods for solving problems. It also provides practice with a variety of problem types and math concepts. For some problems an exact answer is necessary; for others, an estimate is appropriate.

Use this problem set as a review for the *Midyear Test*. Students can work in groups to discuss strategies to solve each problem. (Note that students may be unfamiliar with the word **compost** in *Question 8*. Define compost for them.) You can also use the problems to augment students' homework for the unit. Alternatively, you may choose to use some of the problems as an assessment.

Review Problems

Answer the following questions. You may use any tools that you use in class. For example, you may need to use a ruler, a calculator, or a small centiwheel. You will need graph paper to complete Question 6. Show all your work.

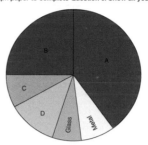

Lin, Irma, Romesh, and John presented this circle graph to their class during a unit on the environment. This graph shows one way experts divide the categories of trash thrown into landfills.

Use this graph to answer Questions 1–5.

1. Organic waste makes up 25% of our trash. What part of the circle graph represents organic waste?

2. We throw away about the same amount of plastic as we do metal. What part of the circle graph represents plastic?

3. Paper makes up between one-third and one-half of our garbage. What part of the circle graph represents paper?

4. There are some things that we throw away that do not fit any of the categories we have listed so far. Examples might include an old telephone or a worn-out chair. This category is labeled miscellaneous. About $\frac{1}{8}$ of the garbage we throw out is considered miscellaneous. What part of the circle graph represents the category miscellaneous?

Student Guide - page 280 (Answers on p. 102)

---

5. About what percent of our trash comes from each category? Use a small centiwheel to help you.

6. Brandon and Roberto discovered an interesting fact while studying recycling: the energy saved from recycling one glass bottle will light a 100-watt bulb for four hours.

    A. Use this fact to complete the data table below. Copy the completed data table on your paper.

N Number of Recycled Glass Bottles	t Time (in hours) a 100-Watt Bulb Can Burn
1	4
3	
	20
7	

    B. Make a graph using your data table.
    C. Use your graph to find how many hours you can light a 100-watt bulb from the energy saved from 4 recycled glass bottles. Show your work on your graph.
    D. If you recycled 10 glass bottles, how many hours can a 100-watt bulb burn with the energy saved? Show your work.
    E. Write a ratio of time to number of glass bottles as a fraction.
    F. Write 2 ratios equivalent to the ratio in Part E.

7. Today, about $\frac{1}{5}$ of our paper is recycled. About what percent of our paper is recycled?

8. Alexis, Felicia, and Ana found that you can compost most organic waste. They learned that 1 pound of red worms will eat 0.5 pound of organic waste each day. The students in Mr. Moreno's class built a worm bin to compost the organic waste from their lunches. The students produce an average of 3.25 pounds of organic waste each week. How many pounds of red worms will they need in their bin if they expect the waste to be fully composted weekly?

Student Guide - page 281 (Answers on pp. 102–103)

Discovery Assignment Book - page 130 (Answers on p. 103)

Homework and Practice

- Assign some or all of the problems for homework.

- Assign Part 6 of the Home Practice, which includes multistep word problems.

Answers for Part 6 of the Home Practice are in the Answer Key at the end of this lesson and at the end of this unit.

Resources

- Appelhoff, Mary, Mary Frances Fenton, and Barbara Loss Harris. *Worms Eat Our Garbage.* Flower Press, Kalamazoo, MI, 1993.

- The EarthWorks Group. *50 Simple Things Kids Can Do to Save the Earth.* Andrews and McMeel, Kansas City, MO, 1999.

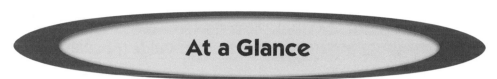
Teaching the Activity

Students solve *Questions 1–8* on the *Review Problems* Activity Pages in the *Student Guide* using calculators, centiwheels, and rulers.

Homework

1. Assign some or all of the problems for review, homework, or use for assessment.
2. Assign Part 6 of the Home Practice.

Answer Key is on pages 102–103.

Notes:

Review Problems

Answer the following questions. You may use any tools that you use in class. For example, you may need to use a ruler, a calculator, or a small centiwheel. You will need graph paper to complete Question 6. Show all your work.

Lin, Irma, Romesh, and John presented this circle graph to their class during a unit on the environment. This graph shows one way experts divide the categories of trash thrown into landfills.

Use this graph to answer Questions 1–5.

1. Organic waste makes up 25% of our trash. What part of the circle graph represents organic waste?

2. We throw away about the same amount of plastic as we do metal. What part of the circle graph represents plastic?

3. Paper makes up between one-third and one-half of our garbage. What part of the circle graph represents paper?

4. There are some things that we throw away that do not fit any of the categories we have listed so far. Examples might include an old telephone or a worn-out chair. This category is labeled miscellaneous. About ⅛ of the garbage we throw out is considered miscellaneous. What part of the circle graph represents the category miscellaneous?

Student Guide - page 280

5. About what percent of our trash comes from each category? Use a small centiwheel to help you.

6. Brandon and Roberto discovered an interesting fact while studying recycling: the energy saved from recycling one glass bottle will light a 100-watt bulb for four hours.

   A. Use this fact to complete the data table below. Copy the completed data table on your paper.

N Number of Recycled Glass Bottles	t Time (in hours) a 100-Watt Bulb Can Burn
1	4
3	
	20
7	

   B. Make a graph using your data table.
   C. Use your graph to find how many hours you can light a 100-watt bulb from the energy saved from 4 recycled glass bottles. Show your work on your graph.
   D. If you recycled 10 glass bottles, how many hours can a 100-watt bulb burn with the energy saved? Show your work.
   E. Write a ratio of time to number of glass bottles as a fraction.
   F. Write 2 ratios equivalent to the ratio in Part E.

7. Today, about ⅕ of our paper is recycled. About what percent of our paper is recycled?

8. Alexis, Felicia, and Ana found that you can compost most organic waste. They learned that 1 pound of red worms will eat 0.5 pound of organic waste each day. The students in Mr. Moreno's class built a worm bin to compost the organic waste from their lunches. The students produce an average of 3.25 pounds of organic waste each week. How many pounds of red worms will they need in their bin if they expect the waste to be fully composted weekly?

Student Guide - page 281

Student Guide (pp. 280–281)

Review Problems

1. purple—B
2. green—C
3. red—A
4. orange—D
5. Part A: About 40%
   Part B: 25%
   Part C: About 8%
   Part D: About 12%
   Glass: About 7%
   Metal: About 8%

6. A.

N Number of Recycled Glass Bottles	t Time (in Hours) a 100-Watt Bulb Can Burn
1	4
3	12
5	20
7	28

B.

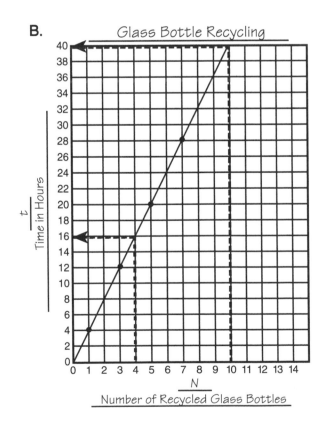

C. 16 hours

D. 40 hours

E. Ratios will vary. One possible ratio is $\frac{4 \text{ hours}}{1 \text{ bottle}}$.

F. Ratios will vary. Two possible ratios are: $\frac{8 \text{ hours}}{2 \text{ bottles}}$ and $\frac{12 \text{ hours}}{3 \text{ bottles}}$.

7. 20%

8. About 6.5 pounds

Discovery Assignment Book (p. 130)

Home Practice*

Part 6. A Birthday Party

1. 60 slices of pizza

2. Answers will vary. Here are some possible combinations and their total cost:

   3 medium and 3 small pizzas ($55.50)

   3 medium, 1 small, and 1 large pizza ($53.50)

   2 large, 2 small, and 1 medium pizza ($54.50)

   5 medium pizzas ($52.50)

   3 large and 1 medium pizza ($52.50)

   4 large pizzas ($56.00)

3. A. 10 children want cheese and sausage

   B. 5 children want cheese

   C. 5 children want pepperoni

4. A. 30 glasses   B. 6 pitchers

   C. $10.50

5. Answers will vary depending on the cheapest order the child finds for **Question 2.** If the total cost for pizza was $52.50 and the total cost of soda was $10.50, then the total cost of the party was $63.00.

6. Answers will vary. Based on the answer in **Question 5:** $37.00

Name _____ Date _____

PART 6 **A Birthday Party**
Solve the following problems. Choose an appropriate method for each: mental math, paper and pencil, or a calculator. Explain your solutions. Use a separate sheet of paper to show your work.

1. Today is Manny's birthday. He invited 19 of his friends to a pizza party at Cheesy Weesy Pizza. Each child will eat 3 slices of pizza. How many slices of pizza will they need? (Don't forget Manny.)

2. The menu reads as follows: Large Pizza (16 slices) $14.00; Medium Pizza (12 slices) $10.50; Small Pizza (8 slices) $8.00. List three possible orders that will feed the 20 children. Which of the three orders is the cheapest?

3. One-half of the children want cheese and sausage pizza. One-fourth want cheese pizza. One-fourth want pepperoni pizza.
   A. How many children want cheese and sausage?
   B. How many want cheese?
   C. How many children want pepperoni?

4. One-half of the children at the party drank two glasses of soda each. The rest drank 1 glass each.
   A. How many total glasses of soda did they drink?
   B. Manny's parents ordered pitchers of soda. If each pitcher of soda serves 5 glasses, how many pitchers were ordered?
   C. If one pitcher costs $1.75, what was the total cost for all of the pitchers of soda?

5. What was the total cost of the party? (Include the cheapest cost of the pizzas and the soda.)

6. Manny's grandfather gave Manny a $100 bill. Manny uses this money to pay for the party. He plans on putting the rest into his savings account. How much will Manny have left for his savings account?

130 DAB • Grade 5 • Unit 8   APPLICATIONS: AN ASSESSMENT UNIT

Discovery Assignment Book - page 130

*Answers for all the Home Practice in the *Discovery Assignment Book* are at the end of the unit.

Lesson 8

Midyear Test

Lesson Overview

Students complete a paper-and-pencil test of 14 items. They will use a calculator, a protractor, and a ruler to complete some of the items. Items are from Units 1–8.

Key Content

• Assessing skills and concepts from the first eight units.

Math Facts

Remind students to study for the *Multiplication and Division Fact Inventory Test.*

Materials List

Supplies and Copies

Student	Teacher
Supplies for Each Student • ruler • calculator • protractor	**Supplies**
Copies • 1 copy of *Centimeter Dot Paper* per student, optional (*Unit Resource Guide* Page 108) • 1 copy of *Midyear Test* per student (*Unit Resource Guide* Pages 109–113)	**Copies/Transparencies**

All blackline masters including assessment, transparency, and DPP masters are also on the Teacher Resource CD.

Daily Practice and Problems and Home Practice

DPP items O–P (*Unit Resource Guide* Pages 22–23)

Note: Classrooms whose pacing differs significantly from the suggested pacing of the units should use the Math Facts Calendar in Section 4 of the *Facts Resource Guide* to ensure students receive the complete math facts program.

Daily Practice and Problems

Suggestions for using the DPPs are on page 106.

O. Bit: Estimating with Money

(URG p. 22)

Estimate the answers to the following problems.

A. $34.56 + $72.35
B. $0.39 + $1.76
C. $0.58 × 8
D. $275.34 − $56.23

Explain your strategy for B.

P. Challenge: Number Puzzles

(URG p. 23)

A. I am 3 tenths less than 5 times 7. Who am I?
B. I am twice the sum of 3.4 and 2.1. Who am I?
C. I am less than 10 but more than 5. If you skip count by two-tenths (.2) starting at 0 you get me. The digit in the ones' place is the same as the digit in the tenths' place. My ones' digit is a multiple of 4.

Teaching the Activity

Students take this test independently. It is designed to take one class period, but make adjustments if needed. Have students complete the first three items (Part 1) without a calculator. They will need a ruler, a protractor, and a calculator to complete Part 2. Make *Centimeter Dot Paper* available, as students may choose to use this to complete **Question 9.**

Remind students to be clear and concise when describing their problem-solving strategies.

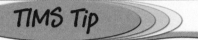

TIMS Tip

Look over the problems before administering the test. If you have not covered the skills required to complete a question, omit it from the test.

Math Facts

Remind students to study the multiplication and division facts at home to prepare for the Inventory Test in DPP item Q in the next lesson.

Extension

Assign DPP Challenge P to students who complete the test early. Item P presents number puzzles that involve decimals.

Math Facts and Daily Practice and Problems

1. Complete DPP items O–P. Bit O involves estimating with money. Challenge P provides number puzzles.
2. Remind students to study for the *Multiplication and Division Fact Inventory Test*.

Teaching the Activity

1. Students solve the first three problems without a calculator.
2. Students complete Part 2 of the test using a ruler, a protractor, and a calculator. Students may also use *Centimeter Dot Paper*.

Extension

Assign DPP Challenge P to students who complete the test early.

Answer Key is on pages 114–116.

Notes:

Centimeter Dot Paper

Blackline Master

Name _____   Date _____

Midyear Test

Part 1

Solve the following problems without using your calculator.

1. There are 5 children in a group. The children have 3275 marbles to share equally. How many marbles will each child get? Show your work.

2. **A.**
    $$694 \\ \underline{\times 8}$$

    B.
    $$83 \\ \underline{\times 27}$$

    C.
    $$2.2 \\ \underline{\times 0.49}$$

    D.
    $$7\overline{)2417}$$

3. Estimate the answers to the following problems.

    A. $697{,}000 \times 20$ **B.** $215{,}000 \div 70$

Name _____ Date _____

Part 2

To answer the questions in Part Two, you may use any tools you use in class. You will need a ruler, a protractor, and a calculator. You may also use *Centimeter Dot Paper.*

4. Write the following number in words.

   3,547,899

5. Find the area of the figure.
   Explain your strategies.
   Give your answer in square centimeters.

   Area =

   Strategies:

6. Complete the table. Write the following fractions as decimals and percents.

Fraction	Decimal	Percent (to the nearest percent)
$\frac{51}{100}$		
$\frac{6}{10}$		
$\frac{3}{50}$		
$\frac{956}{1000}$		

7. John wrote the problem: $1.5 + 2.15 = 2.30$. Nicholas thought John had done the problem wrong. How can Nicholas explain John's mistake?

8. The students at Bessie Coleman Elementary School started a paper
recycling project. Each week, the students collect the used paper from
each classroom. They weigh the paper and then take it to a recycling center.
The students made a graph showing the total amount of paper they recycled
so far. Use the graph to answer the following questions.

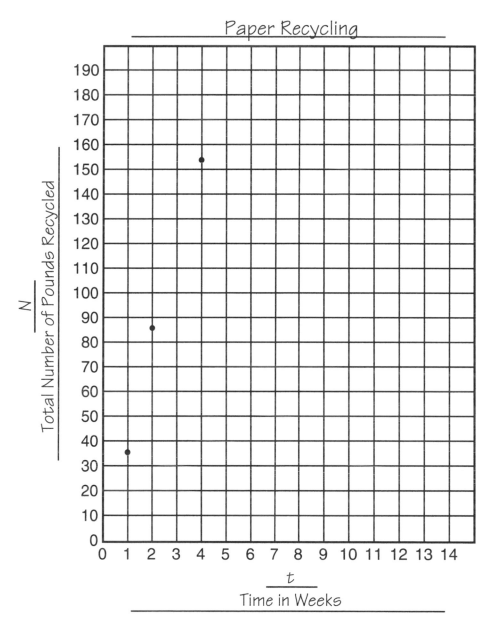

A. Draw a best-fit line.

B. Choose a point on the line and use it to write a fraction to show the ratio of the number of pounds of paper recycled to the time in weeks.

C. For every 117 pounds of paper students recycle, they save an average-size tree. About how many weeks will students have to recycle to save one tree?

D. If there are 36 weeks in the school year, about how many trees can the students save in one school year?

9. Solve the following problems. Show your work.

   A. $\frac{3}{8} + \frac{1}{4} =$

   B. $\frac{7}{10} - \frac{1}{2} =$

10. Use the symbols $<$, $>$, and $=$ to compare these fractions.

   A. $\frac{3}{4}, \frac{9}{12}$

   B. $\frac{1}{2}, \frac{3}{8}$

   C. $\frac{8}{9}, \frac{7}{9}$

   D. $\frac{1}{5}, \frac{1}{3}$

11. Change these mixed numbers to improper fractions.

   A. $1\frac{7}{8}$

   B. $6\frac{4}{9}$

12. Change these fractions to mixed numbers.

   A. $\frac{11}{7}$ **B.** $\frac{23}{5}$

13. Find the sum of the interior angles of this figure. Use any method you wish. Explain your work.

14. Use these measurements to draw quadrilateral ABCD: side AB = 4 cm; angle A = 90 degrees; side DA = 4.7 cm; angle B = 90 degrees; and side BC = 2.5 cm.

   A. What is the length of side DC?

   B. What is the measure of angle C?

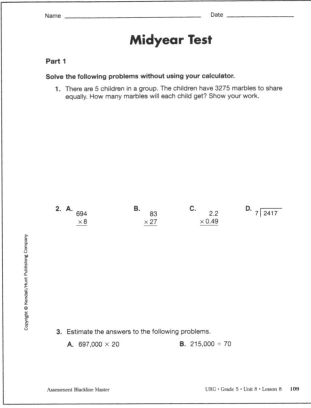

Unit Resource Guide - page 109

Unit Resource Guide (p. 109)

Midyear Test

1. 655 marbles

2. **A.** 5552

   B. 2241

   C. 1.078

   D. 345 R2

3. **A.** Estimates will vary. One possible solution is: 700,000 × 20 = 14,000,000.

   B. Estimates will vary. One possible estimate is: 210,000 ÷ 70 = 3000.

Unit Resource Guide (p. 110)

4. Three million, five hundred forty-seven thousand, eight hundred ninety-nine

5. 12.5 square centimeters; Strategies will vary. Students might measure the length and the width and multiply or they might draw a centimeter grid and count the area.

6. Decimals: 0.51, 0.6, 0.06, 0.956

   Percents: 51%, 60%, 6%, 96%

7. Answers will vary. John added incorrect place values. He added five-tenths to 5 hundredths and one to 1 tenth. By estimating the solution, Nicholas could say that the answer must be bigger than 3 (2 + 1 = 3 and 2.15 + 1.5 must be bigger than 3). The correct answer is 3.65.

Unit Resource Guide - page 110

*Answers and/or discussion are included in the Lesson Guide.

Unit Resource Guide (p. 111)

8. A.

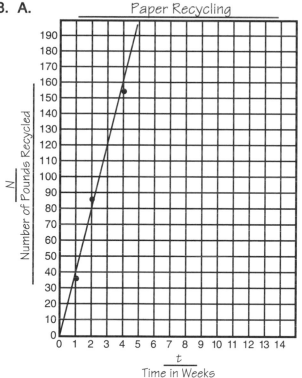

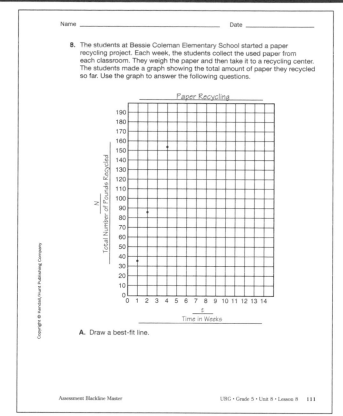

Unit Resource Guide - page 111

Unit Resource Guide (p. 112)

B. Ratios will vary. One possible ratio is $\frac{120 \text{ pounds}}{3 \text{ weeks}}$.

C. About 3 weeks

D. About 12 trees

9. Strategies may vary.

A. $\frac{5}{8}$

B. $\frac{2}{10}$ or $\frac{1}{5}$

10. A. $\frac{3}{4} = \frac{9}{12}$

B. $\frac{1}{2} > \frac{3}{8}$

C. $\frac{8}{9} > \frac{7}{9}$

D. $\frac{1}{5} < \frac{1}{3}$

11. A. $\frac{15}{8}$

B. $\frac{58}{9}$

Unit Resource Guide - page 112

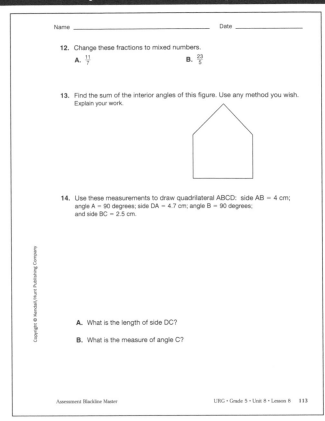

Name _____ Date _____

12. Change these fractions to mixed numbers.

    A. $\frac{11}{7}$ **B.** $\frac{23}{5}$

13. Find the sum of the interior angles of this figure. Use any method you wish. Explain your work.

14. Use these measurements to draw quadrilateral ABCD: side AB = 4 cm; angle A = 90 degrees; side DA = 4.7 cm; angle B = 90 degrees; and side BC = 2.5 cm.

    A. What is the length of side DC?

    B. What is the measure of angle C?

Copyright © Kendall/Hunt Publishing Company

Assessment Blackline Master   URG • Grade 5 • Unit 8 • Lesson 8   113

Unit Resource Guide - page 113

Unit Resource Guide (p. 113)

12. A. $1\frac{4}{7}$

    B. $4\frac{3}{5}$

13. 540°. Explanations will vary. Students may triangulate the pentagon or use a protractor.

14.

D

4.7 cm   C   2.5 cm

A   4 cm   B

A. About 4.5 cm

B. 120°

Lesson 9

Portfolio Review

Lesson Overview

Estimated Class Sessions

1

Students review the work they have collected so far this year to decide which pieces to include in their portfolios.

Key Content

- Using portfolios.
- Reflecting on one's own work.

Math Facts

DPP item Q assesses the multiplication and division facts using an inventory test.

Homework

DPP item R can be assigned as homework.

Assessment

Transfer appropriate documentation from the Unit 8 *Observational Assessment Record* to students' *Individual Assessment Record Sheets.*

Curriculum Sequence

Before This Unit

In Unit 1 students placed completed activities and labs in collection folders in anticipation of choosing work to include in a more formal portfolio. In Unit 2 Lesson 10 students were encouraged to begin a portfolio by choosing pieces from their collection folders. They also started a Table of Contents for their portfolios. Students added work to their collection folders throughout the first seven units. Periodically they chose work from their collection folders to add to their portfolios.

After This Unit

Students will continue to save work in their collection folders as the year progresses. They will review their collection folders periodically and choose pieces for inclusion in student portfolios. Work in the portfolios will show growth over time.

Materials List

Supplies and Copies

Student	Teacher
Supplies for Each Student • collection folder • portfolio folder	**Supplies**
Copies • 1 copy of *Multiplication and Division Fact Inventory Test* per student (*Unit Resource Guide* Page 25)	**Copies/Transparencies**

All blackline masters including assessment, transparency, and DPP masters are also on the Teacher Resource CD.

Student Books
Portfolio Review (*Student Guide* Pages 282–283)

Daily Practice and Problems and Home Practice
DPP items Q–R (*Unit Resource Guide* Pages 23–24)

Note: Classrooms whose pacing differs significantly from the suggested pacing of the units should use the Math Facts Calendar in Section 4 of the *Facts Resource Guide* to ensure students receive the complete math facts program.

Assessment Tools
Observational Assessment Record (*Unit Resource Guide* Pages 11–12)
Individual Assessment Record Sheet (*Teacher Implementation Guide,* Assessment section)

Daily Practice and Problems

Suggestions for using the DPPs are on page 121.

Q. Bit: *Multiplication and Division Fact* *Inventory Test* (URG p. 23)

Students take a test that contains the facts from all five groups of facts studied in Units 2–8—the 5s and 10s, 2s and 3s, square numbers, 9s, and the last six facts.

Students should have two pens or pencils of different colors. During the first four minutes, students write their answers using one color pen or pencil. Encourage students first to answer all the facts they know well and can answer quickly. Then they should go back and use strategies to solve the rest. After four minutes, give students more time to complete the remaining items with the other color pen or pencil.

Using the test results, students should update their new *Multiplication* and *Division Facts I Know* charts.

R. Task: Currency (URG p. 24)

The currency in the European Union is called a Euro. In 2002, 1 Euro was worth 90 cents in the United States. Make a graph to show the number of Euros and their U.S. value. Graph Number of Euros on the horizontal axis and Value in U.S. Dollars and Cents on the vertical axis.

1. How much were 30 Euros worth in U.S. money?
2. If you trade $30.00 of U.S. money for Euros, about how many Euros will you receive?

Portfolio Review

Since the start of the school year, the students in Mr. Moreno's class have collected work for their portfolios. They have saved work that shows what they know, how they solve problems, and how well they can explain their work. Today, the students are updating their portfolios.

"Look through the work in your collection folders," said Mr. Moreno. "Find the activities and labs that best show how you use what you know to solve problems. These are the pieces that you should put in your portfolio. You can compare the work you did earlier this year to the work you are doing now. And don't forget to update your table of contents."

1. If you have not done so recently, choose items from your collection folder to add to your portfolio. Examples of items you might choose are:
   * *Distance vs. Time* from Unit 3
   * *A Day at the Races* from Unit 5
   * *Making Shapes* from Unit 6
   * Work with paper-and-pencil multiplication and division

2. Put your *Experiment Review Chart* from Lesson 1 in your portfolio.

Student Guide - page 282 (Answers on p. 123)

---

3. Choose one or two other pieces of work from this unit to include in your portfolio. Select pieces that are like other work that you put in your portfolio earlier in the year. For example, if you already have a lab in your portfolio, put *Comparing Lives of Animals and Soap Bubbles* in your portfolio, too. Or, if you included a written solution to a problem like *Stack Up*, then also include your writing and graph for *Florence Kelley's Report* in Lesson 4.

4. Add to your Table of Contents. The Table of Contents should include the name of each piece of work, a short description of the work, and the date it was finished.

5. Write a paragraph comparing two pieces of work in your portfolio that are alike in some way. For example, you can compare two labs or your solutions to two problems you have solved. One piece should be new, and one should be from earlier in the year. Here are some questions for you to think about as you write your paragraph:
   * Which two pieces did you choose to compare?
   * How are they alike? How are they different?
   * Do you see any improvement in the newest piece of work as compared to the older work? Explain.
   * If you could redo the older piece of work, how would you improve it?
   * How could you improve the newer piece of work?

6. Write about your favorite piece of work in your portfolio. Tell why you like it. Explain what you learned from it.

Student Guide - page 283 (Answers on p. 123)

Teaching the Activity

This is a good time for students again to review, organize, and add to their portfolios. There are many ways to accomplish this. Specific suggestions for students are on the *Portfolio Review* Assessment Pages in the *Student Guide.* You may follow these suggestions or choose other activities for your students. See the TIMS Tutor: *Portfolios* in the *Teacher Implementation Guide.*

> ## TIMS Tip
>
> The Lesson Guide for Unit 2 Lesson 10 suggested that students focus their portfolios on a specific area such as measurement, graphing, or communication. If there is a focus for the portfolios, review it with your students before they choose pieces to add.

The assessment tasks from previous units as well as this unit make good portfolio entries. Including these tasks in the students' portfolios will allow you, your students, and their parents to assess growth in mathematics learning over time. For example, student performance on the lab *Distance vs. Time* (Unit 3) can be compared to student performance on *A Day at the Races* (Unit 5). Similarly, a student can compare his or her work on the lab *Searching the Forest* (Unit 1) to work on *Comparing Lives of Animals and Soap Bubbles* (Unit 8). By reviewing these labs, improvement in students' abilities to collect, organize, and graph data will be evident. In the same way, look for growth in students' abilities to communicate solutions to problems by comparing student work on earlier assessment tasks to work on *Florence Kelley's Report.* Similar tasks include *Stack Up* from Unit 2 and *Making Shapes* from Unit 6. The *Multiplication and Division Fact Inventory Test* or *Facts I Know* charts are also appropriate entries.

Besides the completed *Experiment Review Chart* from Lesson 1, you may choose at least one more item from this unit that all students will include in their portfolios. Let each student choose one other piece to include. They should place their work in chronological order and update the table of contents. Every two to three weeks, remind students to review their collection folders and portfolios and choose one or two new pieces to include in their portfolios.

TIMS Tip

Keep the number of items in a portfolio manageable. Ten to twelve well-chosen and chronologically arranged pieces per semester may be most useful. To document growth in mathematical learning over time, include similar items from the beginning, middle, and end of the year. Vary the types of assessments.

One way to encourage student reflection is for them to write about the work in their portfolios. *Question 5* in the *Student Guide* asks students to compare two pieces of work in their portfolios. *Question 6* asks each student to write about his or her favorite piece. You can attach students' written responses to these questions to the appropriate labs or activities.

Math Facts

DPP item Q assesses the multiplication and division facts with a short paper-and-pencil test.

Homework and Practice

Assign DPP item R as practice in reading and interpreting line graphs.

Assessment

Transfer appropriate documentation from the Unit 8 *Observational Assessment Record* to students' *Individual Assessment Record Sheets*.

Estimated Class Sessions

1

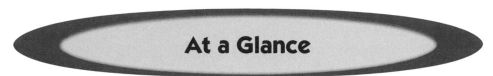

At a Glance

Math Facts and Daily Practice and Problems

Complete DPP items Q–R. Item Q assesses the multiplication and division facts using an inventory test that follows DPP item R.

Teaching the Activity

1. Students review their work in their collection folders and portfolios.
2. Using suggestions on the *Portfolio Review* Activity Pages in the *Student Guide,* students choose activities and labs to include in their portfolios. Other than the *Experiment Review Chart* completed in Lesson 1 of this unit, choose one other piece of work from this unit for all students to include. Have students choose a third item.
3. Students update the table of contents.
4. Students write about the work in their portfolios. See *Questions 5–6* in the *Student Guide.*

Homework

DPP item R can be assigned as homework.

Assessment

Transfer appropriate documentation from the Unit 8 *Observational Assessment Record* to students' *Individual Assessment Record Sheets.*

Answer Key is on page 123.

Notes:

Student Guide (p. 282)

Portfolio Review

Answers will vary.

Portfolio Review

Since the start of the school year, the students in Mr. Moreno's class have collected work for their portfolios. They have saved work that shows what they know, how they solve problems, and how well they can explain their work. Today, the students are updating their portfolios.

"Look through the work in your collection folders," said Mr. Moreno. "Find the activities and labs that best show how you use what you know to solve problems. These are the pieces that you should put in your portfolio. You can compare the work you did earlier this year to the work you are doing now. And don't forget to update your table of contents."

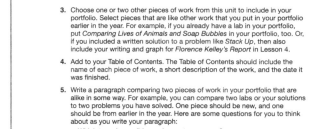

1. If you have not done so recently, choose items from your collection folder to add to your portfolio. Examples of items you might choose are:
    *   *Distance vs. Time* from Unit 3
    *   *A Day at the Races* from Unit 5
    *   *Making Shapes* from Unit 6
    *   Work with paper-and-pencil multiplication and division

2. Put your *Experiment Review Chart* from Lesson 1 in your portfolio.

282   SG • Grade 5 • Unit 8 • Lesson 9   Portfolio Review

Student Guide - page 282

Student Guide (p. 283)

Answers will vary.

---

3. Choose one or two other pieces of work from this unit to include in your portfolio. Select pieces that are like other work that you put in your portfolio earlier in the year. For example, if you already have a lab in your portfolio, put *Comparing Lives of Animals and Soap Bubbles* in your portfolio, too. Or, if you included a written solution to a problem like *Stack Up*, then also include your writing and graph for *Florence Kelley's Report* in Lesson 4.

4. Add to your Table of Contents. The Table of Contents should include the name of each piece of work, a short description of the work, and the date it was finished.

5. Write a paragraph comparing two pieces of work in your portfolio that are alike in some way. For example, you can compare two labs or your solutions to two problems you have solved. One piece should be new, and one should be from earlier in the year. Here are some questions for you to think about as you write your paragraph:
    *   Which two pieces did you choose to compare?
    *   How are they alike? How are they different?
    *   Do you see any improvement in the newest piece of work as compared to the older work? Explain.
    *   If you could redo the older piece of work, how would you improve it?
    *   How could you improve the newer piece of work?

6. Write about your favorite piece of work in your portfolio. Tell why you like it. Explain what you learned from it.

Portfolio Review   SG • Grade 5 • Unit 8 • Lesson 9   283

Student Guide - page 283

Name _____ Date _____

Unit 8 Home Practice

PART 1 *Triangle Flash Cards: All the Facts*

Study for the test on the multiplication and division facts. Take home the flash cards for the facts you need to study.

Ask a family member to choose one flash card at a time. To quiz you on a multiplication fact, he or she should cover the corner containing the highest number. Multiply the two uncovered numbers.

To quiz you on a division fact, your family member can cover one of the smaller numbers. One of the smaller numbers is circled. The other has a square around it. Use the two uncovered numbers to solve a division fact.

Ask your family member to mix up the multiplication and division facts. He or she should sometimes cover the highest number, sometimes cover the circled number, and sometimes cover the number in the square.

Your teacher will tell you when the test on the facts will be given.

PART 2 Practicing the Operations

1. Use paper and pencil to solve the following problems. Estimate each answer to make sure it is reasonable. Show your work on a separate sheet of paper.
   A. $72 \times 61 =$ **B.** $0.43 + 7.6 =$ **C.** $3804 \div 7 =$ **D.** $61 \times 0.29 =$

2. Estimate the following answers. Describe your strategy for each.
   A. $78,000 \div 40$

   B. $104,000 \div 27$

   C. 9821×14

   D. $178 \times 324,000$

APPLICATIONS: AN ASSESSMENT UNIT   DAB • Grade 5 • Unit 8 **127**

Discovery Assignment Book - page 127

Name _____ Date _____

PART 3 Review of Fractions

1. Solve the following problems.
   A. $\frac{7}{8} + \frac{3}{4} =$ **B.** $\frac{5}{6} - \frac{1}{3} =$ **C.** $\frac{11}{12} - \frac{1}{4} =$

2. Change the following mixed numbers to fractions.
   A. $7\frac{1}{3}$ **B.** $3\frac{2}{5}$ **C.** $11\frac{1}{8}$

3. Change the following fractions to mixed numbers.
   A. $\frac{14}{3}$ **B.** $\frac{65}{7}$ **C.** $\frac{103}{10}$

PART 4 Geometry Review

1. Find the area of the shape at the right.

2. What is the measure of $\angle C$? You may use a protractor.

3. What is the measure of $\angle D$? You may use a protractor.

4. A rectangle measures 5.5 cm by 4.6 cm. Is its area greater than or less than the shape above? How do you know?

128 DAB • Grade 5 • Unit 8   APPLICATIONS: AN ASSESSMENT UNIT

Discovery Assignment Book - page 128

Discovery Assignment Book (p. 127)

Part 2. Practicing the Operations

1. **A.** 4392   **B.** 8.03
   C. 543 R3   **D.** 17.69

2. Answers will vary. Possible strategies are shown.
   A. $80,000 \div 40 = 2000$
   B. $100,000 \div 25 = 4000$
   C. $10,000 \times 14 = 140,000$
   D. $200 \times 300,000 = 60,000,000$

Discovery Assignment Book (p. 128)

Part 3. Review of Fractions

1. **A.** $\frac{13}{8}$ or $1\frac{5}{8}$
   B. $\frac{3}{6}$ or $\frac{1}{2}$
   C. $\frac{8}{12}$ or $\frac{2}{3}$

2. **A.** $\frac{22}{3}$
   B. $\frac{17}{5}$
   C. $\frac{89}{8}$

3. **A.** $4\frac{2}{3}$
   B. $9\frac{2}{7}$
   C. $10\frac{3}{10}$

Part 4. Geometry Review

1. 29 sq cm

2. 90°

3. 135°

4. The area of the rectangle is 25.3 sq cm which means it has less area than the shape in *Question 1.* ($5.5 \text{ cm} \times 4.6 \text{ cm} = 25.3 \text{ sq cm}$)

Discovery Assignment Book (pp. 129–130)

Part 5. How Long Are Names?

1. Answers will vary. The graph on the left can be titled "Number of Letters in First Names" and the graph on the right can be titled "Number of Letters in First and Last Names."

2. Answers will vary. Some students may mention that for the data in the graph on the left there is a larger range for the number of letters (10–16 letters) but shorter bars. The graph on the right has a smaller range for the number of letters (4–7) but more data for the numbers within that range (taller bars).

3. Answers will vary. Students will probably mention that the data for the graph on the left shows a larger number of letters in names than the graph on the right. Therefore, the graph on the left shows the letters for first and last names combined.

4. Answers will vary. Possible response: The bars on the graph will be between 3 and 8 letters. The bars will be about twice as tall as the bars on the graph for one class.

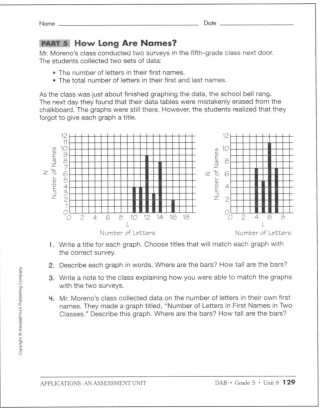

Discovery Assignment Book - page 129

Part 6. A Birthday Party

1. 60 slices of pizza

2. Answers will vary. Here are some possible combinations and their total cost:

   3 medium and 3 small pizzas ($55.50)

   3 medium, 1 small, and 1 large pizza ($53.50)

   2 large, 2 small, and 1 medium pizza ($54.50)

   5 medium pizzas ($52.50)

   3 large and 1 medium pizza ($52.50)

   4 large pizzas ($56.00)

3. **A.** 10 children want cheese and sausage

   B. 5 children want cheese

   C. 5 children want pepperoni

4. **A.** 30 glasses   **B.** 6 pitchers   **C.** $10.50

5. Answers will vary depending on the cheapest order the child finds for *Question 2.* If the total cost for pizza was $52.50 and the total cost of soda was $10.50, then the total cost of the party was $63.00.

6. Answers will vary. Based on the answer in *Question 5:* $37.00

Discovery Assignment Book - page 130

Glossary

This glossary provides definitions of key vocabulary terms in the Grade 5 lessons. Locations of key vocabulary terms in the curriculum are included with each definition. Components Key: URG = *Unit Resource Guide* and SG = *Student Guide.*

A

Acute Angle (URG Unit 6; SG Unit 6)
An angle that measures less than 90°.

Acute Triangle (URG Unit 6 & Unit 15; SG Unit 6 & Unit 15)
A triangle that has only acute angles.

All-Partials Multiplication Method (URG Unit 2)
A paper-and-pencil method for solving multiplication problems. Each partial product is recorded on a separate line. (*See also* partial product.)

$$\begin{array}{r} 186 \\ \times\ 3 \\ \hline 18 \\ 240 \\ 300 \\ \hline 558 \end{array}$$

Altitude of a Triangle (URG Unit 15; SG Unit 15)
A line segment from a vertex of a triangle perpendicular to the opposite side or to the line extending the opposite side; also, the length of this line. The altitude is also called the height of the triangle.

Angle (URG Unit 6; SG Unit 6)
The amount of turning or the amount of opening between two rays that have the same endpoint.

Arc (URG Unit 14; SG Unit 14)
Part of a circle between two points. (*See also* circle.)

Area (URG Unit 4 & Unit 15; SG Unit 4 & Unit 15)
A measurement of size. The area of a shape is the amount of space it covers, measured in square units.

Average (URG Unit 1 & Unit 4; SG Unit 1 & Unit 4)
A number that can be used to represent a typical value in a set of data. (*See also* mean, median, and mode.)

Axes (URG Unit 10; SG Unit 10)
Reference lines on a graph. In the Cartesian coordinate system, the axes are two perpendicular lines that meet at the origin. The singular of axes is axis.

B

Base of a Triangle (URG Unit 15; SG Unit 15)
One of the sides of a triangle; also, the length of the side. A perpendicular line drawn from the vertex opposite the base is called the height or altitude of the triangle.

Base of an Exponent (URG Unit 2; SG Unit 2)
When exponents are used, the number being multiplied. In $3^4 = 3 \times 3 \times 3 \times 3 = 81$, the 3 is the base and the 4 is the exponent. The 3 is multiplied by itself 4 times.

Base-Ten Pieces (URG Unit 2; SG Unit 2)
A set of manipulatives used to model our number system as shown in the figure below. Note that a skinny is made of 10 bits, a flat is made of 100 bits, and a pack is made of 1000 bits.

Base-Ten Shorthand (URG Unit 2)
A graphical representation of the base-ten pieces as shown below.

Nickname	Picture	Shorthand
bit	⬜	·
skinny	▭▭▭▭▭	/
flat		⬜
pack		⬜

Benchmarks (SG Unit 7)
Numbers convenient for comparing and ordering numbers, e.g., $0, \frac{1}{2}, 1$ are convenient benchmarks for comparing and ordering fractions.

Best-Fit Line (URG Unit 3; SG Unit 3)
The line that comes closest to the points on a point graph.

Binning Data (URG Unit 8; SG Unit 8)
Placing data from a data set with a large number of values or large range into intervals in order to more easily see patterns in the data.

Bit (URG Unit 2; SG Unit 2)
A cube that measures 1 cm on each edge.
It is the smallest of the base-ten pieces and is often used to represent 1. (*See also* base-ten pieces.)

C

Cartesian Coordinate System (URG Unit 10; SG Unit 10)
A method of locating points on a flat surface by means of an ordered pair of numbers. This method is named after its originator, René Descartes. (*See also* coordinates.)

Categorical Variable (URG Unit 1; SG Unit 1)
Variables with values that are not numbers. (*See also* variable and value.)

Center of a Circle (URG Unit 14; SG Unit 14)
The point such that every point on a circle is the same distance from it. (*See also* circle.)

Centiwheel (URG Unit 7; SG Unit 7)
A circle divided into 100 equal sections used in exploring fractions, decimals, and percents.

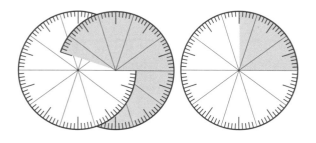

Central Angle (URG Unit 14; SG Unit 14)
An angle whose vertex is at the center of a circle.

Certain Event (URG Unit 7; SG Unit 7)
An event that has a probability of 1 (100%).

Chord (URG Unit 14; SG Unit 14)
A line segment that connects two points on a circle. (*See also* circle.)

Circle (URG Unit 14; SG Unit 14)
A curve that is made up of all the points that are the same distance from one point, the center.

Circumference (URG Unit 14; SG Unit 14)
The distance around a circle.

Common Denominator (URG Unit 5 & Unit 11; SG Unit 5 & Unit 11)
A denominator that is shared by two or more fractions. A common denominator is a common multiple of the denominators of the fractions. 15 is a common denominator of $\frac{2}{3}$ ($= \frac{10}{15}$) and $\frac{4}{5}$ ($= \frac{12}{15}$) since 15 is divisible by both 3 and 5.

Common Fraction (URG Unit 7; SG Unit 7)
Any fraction that is written with a numerator and denominator that are whole numbers. For example, $\frac{3}{4}$ and $\frac{9}{4}$ are both common fractions. (*See also* decimal fraction.)

Commutative Property of Addition (URG Unit 2)
The order of the addends in an addition problem does not matter, e.g., $7 + 3 = 3 + 7$.

Commutative Property of Multiplication (URG Unit 2)
The order of the factors in a multiplication problem does not matter, e.g., $7 \times 3 = 3 \times 7$. (*See also* turn-around facts.)

Compact Method (URG Unit 2)
Another name for what is considered the traditional multiplication algorithm.

$$\begin{array}{r} {\overset{2}{}\overset{1}{1}86} \\ \times\ 3 \\ \hline 558 \end{array}$$

Composite Number (URG Unit 11; SG Unit 11)
A number that has more than two distinct factors. For example, 9 has three factors (1, 3, 9) so it is a composite number.

Concentric Circles (URG Unit 14; SG Unit 14)
Circles that have the same center.

Congruent (URG Unit 6 & Unit 10; SG Unit 6)
Figures that are the same shape and size. Polygons are congruent when corresponding sides have the same length and corresponding angles have the same measure.

Conjecture (URG Unit 11; SG Unit 11)
A statement that has not been proved to be true, nor shown to be false.

Convenient Number (URG Unit 2; SG Unit 2)
A number used in computation that is close enough to give a good estimate, but is also easy to compute with mentally, e.g., 25 and 30 are convenient numbers for 27.

Convex (URG Unit 6)
A shape is convex if for any two points in the shape, the line segment between the points is also inside the shape.

Coordinates (URG Unit 10; SG Unit 10)
An ordered pair of numbers that locates points on a flat surface relative to a pair of coordinate axes. For example, in the ordered pair (4, 5), the first number (coordinate) is the distance from the point to the vertical axis and the second coordinate is the distance from the point to the horizontal axis. (*See also* axes.)

Corresponding Parts (URG Unit 10; SG Unit 10)
Matching parts in two or more figures. In the figure below, Sides AB and A′B′ are corresponding parts.

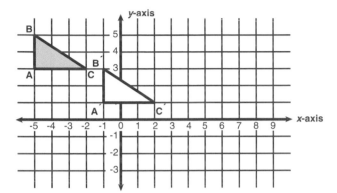

Cryptography (SG Unit 11) The study of secret codes.

Cubic Centimeter (URG Unit 13)
The volume of a cube that is one centimeter long on each edge.

D

Data (SG Unit 1)
Information collected in an experiment or survey.

Decagon (URG Unit 6; SG Unit 6)
A ten-sided, ten-angled polygon.

Decimal (URG Unit 7; SG Unit 7)
1. A number written using the base ten place value system.
2. A number containing a decimal point.

Decimal Fraction (URG Unit 7; SG Unit 7)
A fraction written as a decimal. For example, 0.75 and 0.4 are decimal fractions and $\frac{75}{100}$ and $\frac{4}{10}$ are the equivalent common fractions.

Degree (URG Unit 6; SG Unit 6)
A degree (°) is a unit of measure for angles. There are 360 degrees in a circle.

Denominator (URG Unit 3; SG Unit 3)
The number below the line in a fraction. The denominator indicates the number of equal parts in which the unit whole is divided. For example, the 5 is the denominator in the fraction $\frac{2}{5}$. In this case the unit whole is divided into five equal parts. (*See also* numerator.)

Density (URG Unit 13; SG Unit 13)
The ratio of an object's mass to its volume.

Diagonal (URG Unit 6)
A line segment that connects nonadjacent corners of a polygon.

Diameter (URG Unit 14; SG Unit 14)
1. A line segment that connects two points on a circle and passes through the center.
2. The length of this line segment.

Digit (SG Unit 2)
Any one of the ten symbols 0, 1, 2, 3, 4, 5, 6, 7, 8, 9. The number 37 is made up of the digits 3 and 7.

Dividend (URG Unit 4 & Unit 9; SG Unit 4 & Unit 9)
The number that is divided in a division problem, e.g., 12 is the dividend in $12 \div 3 = 4$.

Divisor (URG Unit 2, Unit 4, & Unit 9; SG Unit 2, Unit 4, & Unit 9)
In a division problem, the number by which another number is divided. In the problem $12 \div 4 = 3$, the 4 is the divisor, the 12 is the dividend, and the 3 is the quotient.

Dodecagon (URG Unit 6; SG Unit 6)
A twelve-sided, twelve-angled polygon.

E

Endpoint (URG Unit 6; SG Unit 6)
The point at either end of a line segment or the point at the end of a ray.

Equally Likely (URG Unit 7; SG Unit 7)
When events have the same probability, they are called equally likely.

Equidistant (URG Unit 14)
At the same distance.

Equilateral Triangle (URG Unit 6, Unit 14, & Unit 15)
A triangle that has all three sides equal in length. An equilateral triangle also has three equal angles.

Equivalent Fractions (URG Unit 3; SG Unit 3)
Fractions that have the same value, e.g., $\frac{2}{4} = \frac{1}{2}$.

Estimate (URG Unit 2; SG Unit 2)
1. To find *about* how many (as a verb).
2. A number that is *close to* the desired number (as a noun).

Expanded Form (SG Unit 2)
A way to write numbers that shows the place value of each digit, e.g., $4357 = 4000 + 300 + 50 + 7$.

Exponent (URG Unit 2 & Unit 11; SG Unit 2 & Unit 11)
The number of times the base is multiplied by itself. In $3^4 = 3 \times 3 \times 3 \times 3 = 81$, the 3 is the base and the 4 is the exponent. The 3 is multiplied by itself 4 times.

Extrapolation (URG Unit 13; SG Unit 13)
Using patterns in data to make predictions or to estimate values that lie beyond the range of values in the set of data.

F

Fact Families (URG Unit 2; SG Unit 2)
Related math facts, e.g., $3 \times 4 = 12$, $4 \times 3 = 12$, $12 \div 3 = 4$, $12 \div 4 = 3$.

Factor Tree (URG Unit 11; SG Unit 11)
A diagram that shows the prime factorization of a number.

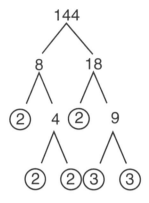

Factors (URG Unit 2 & Unit 11; SG Unit 2 & Unit 11)
1. In a multiplication problem, the numbers that are multiplied together. In the problem $3 \times 4 = 12$, 3 and 4 are the factors.
2. Numbers that divide a number evenly, e.g., 1, 2, 3, 4, 6, and 12 are all the factors of 12.

Fair Game (URG Unit 7; SG Unit 7)
A game in which it is equally likely that any player will win.

Fewest Pieces Rule (URG Unit 2)
Using the least number of base-ten pieces to represent a number. (*See also* base-ten pieces.)

Fixed Variables (URG Unit 4; SG Unit 3 & Unit 4)
Variables in an experiment that are held constant or not changed, in order to find the relationship between the manipulated and responding variables. These variables are often called controlled variables. (*See also* manipulated variable and responding variable.)

Flat (URG Unit 2; SG Unit 2)
A block that measures 1 cm × 10 cm × 10 cm. It is one of the base-ten pieces and is often used to represent 100. (*See also* base-ten pieces.)

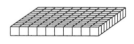

Flip (URG Unit 10; SG Unit 10)
A motion of the plane in which the plane is reflected over a line so that any point and its image are the same distance from the line.

Forgiving Division Method
   (URG Unit 4; SG Unit 4)
A paper-and-pencil method for division in which successive partial quotients are chosen and subtracted from the dividend, until the remainder is less than the divisor. The sum of the partial quotients is the quotient. For example, $644 \div 7$ can be solved as shown at the right.

```
        92
   7 )644
      140  20
      504
      350  50
      154
      140  20
       14
       14   2
        0  92
```

Formula (SG Unit 11 & Unit 14)
A number sentence that gives a general rule. A formula for finding the area of a rectangle is Area = length × width, or $A = l \times w$.

Fraction (URG Unit 7; SG Unit 7)
A number that can be written as a/b where a and b are whole numbers and b is not zero.

G

Googol (URG Unit 2)
A number that is written as a 1 with 100 zeroes after it (10^{100}).

Googolplex (URG Unit 2)
A number that is written as a 1 with a googol of zeroes after it.

H

Height of a Triangle (URG Unit 15; SG Unit 15)
A line segment from a vertex of a triangle perpendicular to the opposite side or to the line extending the opposite side; also, the length of this line. The height is also called the altitude.

Hexagon (URG Unit 6; SG Unit 6)
A six-sided polygon.

Hypotenuse (URG Unit 15; SG Unit 15)
The longest side of a right triangle.

I

Image (URG Unit 10; SG Unit 10)
The result of a transformation, in particular a slide (translation) or a flip (reflection), in a coordinate plane. The new figure after the slide or flip is the image of the old figure.

Impossible Event (URG Unit 7; SG Unit 7)
An event that has a probability of 0 or 0%.

Improper Fraction (URG Unit 3; SG Unit 3)
A fraction in which the numerator is greater than or equal to the denominator. An improper fraction is greater than or equal to one.

Infinite (URG Unit 2)
Never ending, immeasurably great, unlimited.

Interpolation (URG Unit 13; SG Unit 13)
Making predictions or estimating values that lie between data points in a set of data.

Intersect (URG Unit 14)
To meet or cross.

Isosceles Triangle (URG Unit 6 & Unit 15)
A triangle that has at least two sides of equal length.

J

K

L

Lattice Multiplication
(URG Unit 9; SG Unit 9)
A method for multiplying that
uses a lattice to arrange the
partial products so the digits are
correctly placed in the correct
place value columns. A lattice
for 43 × 96 = 4128 is shown at
the right.

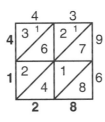

Legs of a Right Triangle (URG Unit 15; SG Unit 15)
The two sides of a right triangle that form the right angle.

Length of a Rectangle (URG Unit 4 & Unit 15;
SG Unit 4 & Unit 15)
The distance along one side of a rectangle.

Line
A set of points that form a straight path extending infinitely in two directions.

Line of Reflection (URG Unit 10)
A line that acts as a mirror so that after a shape is flipped over the line, corresponding points are at the same distance (equidistant) from the line.

Line Segment (URG Unit 14)
A part of a line between and including two points, called the endpoints.

Liter (URG Unit 13)
Metric unit used to measure volume. A liter is a little more than a quart.

Lowest Terms (SG Unit 11)
A fraction is in lowest terms if the numerator and denominator have no common factor greater than 1.

M

Manipulated Variable (URG Unit 4; SG Unit 4)
In an experiment, the variable with values known at the beginning of the experiment. The experimenter often chooses these values before data is collected. The manipulated variable is often called the independent variable.

Mass (URG Unit 13)
The amount of matter in an object.

Mean (URG Unit 1 & Unit 4; SG Unit 1 & Unit 4)
An average of a set of numbers that is found by adding the values of the data and dividing by the number of values.

Measurement Division (URG Unit 4)
Division as equal grouping. The total number of objects and the number of objects in each group are known. The number of groups is the unknown. For example, tulip bulbs come in packages of 8. If 216 bulbs are sold, how many packages are sold?

Median (URG Unit 1; SG Unit 1)
For a set with an odd number of data arranged in order, it is the middle number. For an even number of data arranged in order, it is the mean of the two middle numbers.

Meniscus (URG Unit 13)
The curved surface formed when a liquid creeps up the side of a container (for example, a graduated cylinder).

Milliliter (ml) (URG Unit 13)
A measure of capacity in the metric system that is the volume of a cube that is one centimeter long on each side.

Mixed Number (URG Unit 3; SG Unit 3)
A number that is written as a whole number followed by a fraction. It is equal to the sum of the whole number and the fraction.

Mode (URG Unit 1; SG Unit 1)
The most common value in a data set.

Mr. Origin (URG Unit 10; SG Unit 10)
A plastic figure used to represent the origin of a coordinate system and to indicate the directions of the x- and y- axes. (and possibly the z-axis).

N

N-gon (URG Unit 6; SG Unit 6)
A polygon with N sides.

Negative Number (URG Unit 10; SG Unit 10)
A number less than zero; a number to the left of zero on a horizontal number line.

Nonagon (URG Unit 6; SG Unit 6)
A nine-sided polygon.

Numerator (URG Unit 3; SG Unit 3)
The number written above the line in a fraction. For example, the 2 is the numerator in the fraction $\frac{2}{5}$. In this case, we are interested in two of the five parts. (*See also* denominator.)

Numerical Expression (URG Unit 4; SG Unit 4)
A combination of numbers and operations, e.g.,
$5 + 8 \div 4$.

Numerical Variable (URG Unit 1; SG Unit 1)
Variables with values that are numbers. (*See also* variable and value.)

O

Obtuse Angle (URG Unit 6; SG Unit 6)
An angle that measures more than 90°.

Obtuse Triangle (URG Unit 6 & Unit 15; SG Unit 6 & Unit 15)
A triangle that has an obtuse angle.

Octagon (URG Unit 6; SG Unit 6)
An eight-sided polygon.

Ordered Pair (URG Unit 10; SG Unit 10)
A pair of numbers that gives the coordinates of a point on a grid in relation to the origin. The horizontal coordinate is given first; the vertical coordinate is given second. For example, the ordered pair (5, 3) gives the coordinates of the point that is 5 units to the right of the origin and 3 units up.

Origin (URG Unit 10; SG Unit 10)
The point at which the *x*- and *y*-axes intersect on a coordinate plane. The origin is described by the ordered pair (0, 0) and serves as a reference point so that all the points on the plane can be located by ordered pairs.

P

Pack (URG Unit 2; SG Unit 2)
A cube that measures 10 cm on each edge. It is one of the base-ten pieces and is often used to represent 1000. (*See also* base-ten pieces.)

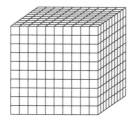

Parallel Lines
(URG Unit 6 & Unit 10)
Lines that are in the same direction. In the plane, parallel lines are lines that do not intersect.

Parallelogram (URG Unit 6)
A quadrilateral with two pairs of parallel sides.

Partial Product (URG Unit 2)
One portion of the multiplication process in the all-partials multiplication method, e.g., in the problem 3 × 186 there are three partial products: 3 × 6 = 18, 3 × 80 = 240, and 3 × 100 = 300. (*See also* all-partials multiplication method.)

Partitive Division (URG Unit 4)
Division as equal sharing. The total number of objects and the number of groups are known. The number of objects in each group is the unknown. For example, Frank has 144 marbles that he divides equally into 6 groups. How many marbles are in each group?

Pentagon (URG Unit 6; SG Unit 6)
A five-sided polygon.

Percent (URG Unit 7; SG Unit 7)
Per hundred or out of 100. A special ratio that compares a number to 100. For example, 20% (twenty percent) of the jelly beans are yellow means that out of every 100 jelly beans, 20 are yellow.

Perimeter (URG Unit 15; SG Unit 15)
The distance around a two-dimensional shape.

Period (SG Unit 2)
A group of three places in a large number, starting on the right, often separated by commas as shown at the right.

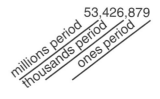

Perpendicular Lines (URG Unit 14 & Unit 15; SG Unit 14)
Lines that meet at right angles.

Pi (π) (URG Unit 14; SG Unit 14)
The ratio of the circumference to diameter of a circle. π = 3.14159265358979. . . . It is a nonterminating, nonrepeating decimal.

Place (SG Unit 2)
The position of a digit in a number.

Place Value (URG Unit 2; SG Unit 2)
The value of a digit in a number. For example, the 5 is in the hundreds place in 4573, so it stands for 500.

Polygon (URG Unit 6; SG Unit 6)
A two-dimensional connected figure made of line segments in which each endpoint of every side meets with an endpoint of exactly one other side.

Population (URG Unit 1 Unit 1)
A collection of persons or things whose properties will be analyzed in a survey or experiment.

Portfolio (URG Unit 2; SG Unit 2)
A collection of student work that show how a student's skills, attitudes, and knowledge change over time.

Positive Number (URG Unit 10; SG Unit 10)
A number greater than zero; a number to the right of zero on a horizontal number line.

Power (URG Unit 2; SG Unit 2)
An exponent. Read 10^4 as, "ten to the fourth power" or "ten to the fourth." We say 10,000 or 10^4 is the fourth power of ten.

Prime Factorization (URG Unit 11; SG Unit 11)
Writing a number as a product of primes. The prime factorization of 100 is 2 × 2 × 5 × 5.

Prime Number (URG Unit 11; SG Unit 11)
A number that has exactly two factors: itself and 1. For example, 7 has exactly two distinct factors, 1 and 7.

Probability (URG Unit 7; SG Unit 1 & Unit 7)
A number from 0 to 1 (0% to 100%) that describes how likely an event is to happen. The closer that the probability of an event is to one, the more likely the event will happen.

Product (URG Unit 2; SG Unit 2)
The answer to a multiplication problem. In the problem $3 \times 4 = 12$, 12 is the product.

Proper Fraction (URG Unit 3; SG Unit 3)
A fraction in which the numerator is less than the denominator. Proper fractions are less than one.

Proportion (URG Unit 3 & Unit 13; SG Unit 13)
A statement that two ratios are equal.

Protractor (URG Unit 6; SG Unit 6)
A tool for measuring angles.

Q

Quadrants (URG Unit 10; SG Unit 10)
The four sections of a coordinate grid that are separated by the axes.

Quadrilateral (URG Unit 6; SG Unit 6)
A polygon with four sides. (*See also* polygon.)

Quotient (URG Unit 4 & Unit 9; SG Unit 2, Unit 4, & Unit 9)
The answer to a division problem. In the problem $12 \div 3 = 4$, the 4 is the quotient.

R

Radius (URG Unit 14; SG Unit 14)
1. A line segment connecting the center of a circle to any point on the circle.
2. The length of this line segment.

Ratio (URG Unit 3 & Unit 12; SG Unit 3 & Unit 13)
A way to compare two numbers or quantities using division. It is often written as a fraction.

Ray (URG Unit 6; SG Unit 6)
A part of a line with one endpoint that extends indefinitely in one direction.

Rectangle (URG Unit 6; SG Unit 6)
A quadrilateral with four right angles.

Reflection (URG Unit 10)
(*See* flip.)

Regular Polygon (URG Unit 6; SG Unit 6; DAB Unit 6)
A polygon with all sides of equal length and all angles equal.

Remainder (URG Unit 4 & Unit 9; SG Unit 4 & Unit 9)
Something that remains or is left after a division problem. The portion of the dividend that is not evenly divisible by the divisor, e.g., $16 \div 5 = 3$ with 1 as a remainder.

Repeating Decimals (SG Unit 9)
A decimal fraction with one or more digits repeating without end.

Responding Variable (URG Unit 4; SG Unit 4)
The variable whose values result from the experiment. Experimenters find the values of the responding variable by doing the experiment. The responding variable is often called the dependent variable.

Rhombus (URG Unit 6; SG Unit 6)
A quadrilateral with four equal sides.

Right Angle (URG Unit 6; SG Unit 6)
An angle that measures 90°.

Right Triangle (URG Unit 6 & Unit 15; SG Unit 6 & Unit 15)
A triangle that contains a right angle.

Rubric (URG Unit 1)
A scoring guide that can be used to guide or assess student work.

S

Sample (URG Unit 1)
A part or subset of a population.

Scalene Triangle (URG Unit 15)
A triangle that has no sides that are equal in length.

Scientific Notation (URG Unit 2; SG Unit 2)
A way of writing numbers, particularly very large or very small numbers. A number in scientific notation has two factors. The first factor is a number greater than or equal to one and less than ten. The second factor is a power of 10 written with an exponent. For example, 93,000,000 written in scientific notation is 9.3×10^7.

Septagon (URG Unit 6; SG Unit 6)
A seven-sided polygon.

Side-Angle-Side (URG Unit 6 & Unit 14)
A geometric property stating that two triangles having two corresponding sides with the included angle equal are congruent.

Side-Side-Side (URG Unit 6)
A geometric property stating that two triangles having corresponding sides equal are congruent.

Sides of an Angle (URG Unit 6; SG Unit 6)
The sides of an angle are two rays with the same endpoint. (*See also* endpoint and ray.)

Sieve of Eratosthenes (SG Unit 11)
A method for separating prime numbers from nonprime numbers developed by Eratosthenes, an Egyptian librarian, in about 240 BCE.

Similar (URG Unit 6; SG Unit 6)
Similar shapes have the same shape but not necessarily the same size.

Skinny (URG Unit 2; SG Unit 2)
A block that measures 1 cm × 1 cm × 10 cm.
It is one of the base-ten pieces
and is often used to represent 10.
(*See also* base-ten pieces.)

Slide (URG Unit 10; SG Unit 10)
Moving a geometric figure in the plane by moving every point of the figure the same distance in the same direction. Also called translation.

Speed (URG Unit 3 & Unit 5; SG Unit 3 & Unit 5)
The ratio of distance moved to time taken, e.g.,
3 miles/1 hour or 3 mph is a speed.

Square (URG Unit 6 & Unit 14; SG Unit 6)
A quadrilateral with four equal sides and four right angles.

Square Centimeter (URG Unit 4; SG Unit 4)
The area of a square that is 1 cm long on each side.

Square Number (URG Unit 11)
A number that is the product of a whole number multiplied by itself. For example, 25 is a square number since
$5 \times 5 = 25$. A square number can be represented by a square array with the same number of rows as columns. A square array for 25 has 5 rows of 5 objects in each row or 25 total objects.

Standard Form (SG Unit 2)
The traditional way to write a number, e.g., standard form for three hundred fifty-seven is 357. (*See also* expanded form and word form.)

Standard Units (URG Unit 4)
Internationally or nationally agreed-upon units used in measuring variables, e.g., centimeters and inches are standard units used to measure length and square centimeters and square inches are used to measure area.

Straight Angle (URG Unit 6; SG Unit 6)
An angle that measures 180°.

T

Ten Percent (URG Unit 4; SG Unit 4)
10 out of every hundred or $\frac{1}{10}$.

Tessellation (URG Unit 6 & Unit 10; SG Unit 6)
A pattern made up of one or more repeated shapes that completely covers a surface without any gaps or overlaps.

Translation
(*See* slide.)

Trapezoid (URG Unit 6)
A quadrilateral with exactly one pair of parallel sides.

Triangle (URG Unit 6; SG Unit 6)
A polygon with three sides.

Triangulating (URG Unit 6; SG Unit 6)
Partitioning a polygon into two or more nonoverlapping triangles by drawing diagonals that do not intersect.

Turn-Around Facts (URG Unit 2)
Multiplication facts that have the same factors but in a different order, e.g., $3 \times 4 = 12$ and $4 \times 3 = 12$.
(*See also* commutative property of multiplication.)

Twin Primes (URG Unit 11; SG Unit 11)
A pair of prime numbers whose difference is 2.
For example, 3 and 5 are twin primes.

U

Unit Ratio (URG Unit 13; SG Unit 13)
A ratio with a denominator of one.

V

Value (URG Unit 1; SG Unit 1)
The possible outcomes of a variable. For example, red, green, and blue are possible values for the variable *color.* Two meters and 1.65 meters are possible values for the variable *length.*

Variable (URG Unit 1; SG Unit 1)
1. An attribute or quantity that changes or varies.
   (*See also* categorical variable and numerical variable.)
2. A symbol that can stand for a variable.

Variables in Proportion (URG Unit 13; SG Unit 13)
When the ratio of two variables in an experiment is always the same, the variables are in proportion.

Velocity (URG Unit 5; SG Unit 5)
Speed in a given direction. Speed is the ratio of the distance traveled to time taken.

Vertex (URG Unit 6; SG Unit 6)
A common point of two rays or line segments that form an angle.

Volume (URG Unit 13)
The measure of the amount of space occupied by an object.

W

Whole Number
Any of the numbers 0, 1, 2, 3, 4, 5, 6 and so on.

Width of a Rectangle (URG Unit 4 & Unit 15;
    SG Unit 4 & Unit 15)
The distance along one side of a rectangle is the length and the distance along an adjacent side is the width.

Word Form (SG Unit 2)
A number expressed in words, e.g., the word form for 123 is "one hundred twenty-three." (*See also* expanded form and standard form.)

X

Y

Z